DATE DUE

MY 12 '95			
MY 24 '96			
DE 18 '98			
OC 18 '99			
~~SE 27 02~~			

DEMCO 38-296

Behavior
Modification

Behavior Modification

William M. Sherman, Ph.D.
Center for Behavior Therapy and Health Psychology,
New Haven, Connecticut

HARPER & ROW, PUBLISHERS, New York
Grand Rapids, Philadelphia, St. Louis, San Francisco,
London, Singapore, Sydney, Tokyo

Sponsoring Editor: Laura Pearson
Project Editor: Carla Samodulski
Art Direction: Heather Ziegler
Cover Coordinator: Mary Archondes
Cover Design: Wanda Lubelska Design
Production: Willie Lane

BEHAVIOR MODIFICATION

Library of Congress Cataloging-in-Publication Data

Sherman, William M.
    Behavior modification.

    Bibliography: p.
    Includes index.
    1. Behavior modification.   I. Title.
BF637.B4S59   1990   616.89′142   89-11207
ISBN 0-06-046105-5

    90 91 92 9 8 7 6 5 4 3 2

I respectfully dedicate this book to the memory of my parents; they would have been proud.

Contents

Preface

When I interviewed for my first full-time teaching position, I was asked if I could teach an undergraduate course in behavior modification. I remember thinking how few appropriate texts there were in those days and wondering whether I could stretch the material I had to cover a whole semester. The times have certainly changed. The field of behavior modification has evolved and developed, and I have learned much. I now worry if I only have one semester to present all the material that is available.

It is within this context that I was eager to write this book. From the start, my intent was to provide an introductory-level book that would be at the same time both complete and concise. Because I find myself teaching the principles and procedures of behavior modification in a variety of different courses and to students with many different backgrounds and interests, I wanted this text to have as broad an appeal as possible. While it could stand alone and serve as the main text in some courses, it could also serve as a supplementary text where the professor wishes either to review or to emphasize the behavioral approach to clinical psychology. Where the book is to be used as a main text, it is well referenced, and the student can delve deeper; where it is to be used as a supplementary text, it provides a solid overview. Finally, I have tried to give the text a practical and useful orientation based on the model of behavior modification I know best, that of a practitioner in private practice.

I hope I have succeeded in fulfilling these intentions. Where I have not, the fault is solely mine. Where I have, the credit must be shared. I would like to give my thanks to a number of people: to Madeleine Leveille, Leslie Weiss, and Reid Daitzman for their thoughtful reviews of an earlier (much earlier) version of the manuscript; Ellen Davis for both her encouragement and very skillful secretarial assistance; the Harper & Row editors and the following reviewers, whose efforts have made this a better book:

Roger McIntyre
University of Maryland

John Steffen
University of Cincinnati

Julian Streitfeld
University of Hartford

Robert Goodkin
Montclair State College

Wilma Henzlik
Wright State University

Max Brill
Oakland University

Gary Brown
University of Tennessee

David Lutz
Southwest Missouri State University

Charles Frederickson
Centenary College

Warren Tryon
Fordham University

I would like to thank my patients, whom I have taught and from whom I have learned. Finally, to my daughters Alison and Jaime, for understanding why I spent all those evenings and weekends "in the basement," and to my wife Wendy, for her constant support, expertise, time, and effort, I owe much and give my love.

William M. Sherman

About the Author

William M. Sherman received his doctorate from New York University and postdoctoral specialty training from the Center for Behavioral Psychotherapy. He has taught at New York University, the City University of New York, the University of Bridgeport, Southern Connecticut State University, and Albertus Magnus College, where he was the chairperson of the Department of Psychology. He is a member of the American Psychological Association and the Association for Advancement of Behavior Therapy. Dr. Sherman has also served as president of the Connecticut Behavior Therapy Association and is a diplomate of the American Board of Medical Psychotherapists. He is currently in private practice with the Center for Behavior Therapy and Health Psychology in New Haven, Connecticut.

Behavior Modification

Introduction

This textbook introduces the student to the clinical procedures and techniques subsumed under the broad title of **behavior modification**. The orientation presented is the *operant conditioning* model of learning—that is, the systematic manipulation of *contingencies* and *consequences*. These therapeutic interventions use *rewards* and *punishments* to *increase desirable behaviors* and *decrease undesirable behaviors* and are often referred to as **contingency management**.

Behavior modification in general, and contingency management in particular, have applications both within the realm of mental health and outside of it. Kazdin (1978) claims that "treatment programs based on principles of operant conditioning have been extended to almost every type of treatment, educational, and health care facility from preschools to nursing homes, as well as to client populations ranging from psychiatric patients to the mentally retarded. Within behavior modification, no single conceptual and experimental approach has generated the breadth of application that operant conditioning has" (p. x). Operant conditioning and contingency management have even found their way into the rules, morals, and lessons of familiar children's games. Included in the description of and rules for the board game "Chutes and Ladders" (Milton Bradley Co.), for example, is the statement: ". . . In going up the ladders and down the chutes, a child will learn by the pictures the rewards of good deeds and the consequences of naughty ones."

In an issue of *The Behavior Therapist*, Wade, Baker, & Hartmann (1979) report the results of a survey they administered to 257 randomly selected members of the Association for Advancement of Behavior Therapy (AABT). One of the questions on the survey assessed commonly used treatment procedures. Operant conditioning techniques were used by the largest number of therapists (60.7 percent) with the greatest percentage of clients (31.9 percent). When one considers additionally such other operant techniques as behavioral contracts (used by 11.3 percent of therapists and 3.8 percent of clients) and behavioral rehearsal (9.3 percent of therapists; 3.8 percent of clients), the dramatic impact of operant conditioning on behavior modification becomes still more striking.

ACCEPTANCE OF BEHAVIOR MODIFICATION

Although there are a number of theoretical or philosophical positions or points of view within clinical psychology (e.g., behavioral, psychodynamic, Rogerian, transactional, Gestalt, and so on), behavior modification appears to be gaining rapidly in both acceptance and popularity. Thyer (1987a) discusses the acceptance of the behavioral approach in the field of clinical social work. According to a national survey he conducted on graduate social work curricula, the majority of the surveyed programs now offer some coursework in behavioral methods. Referring to a survey by Jayaratne (1978), Thyer reports that "behavior therapy/learning theory is a preferred theoretical orientation . . . [in] about one-third of surveyed clinical social workers" (p. 132). In conclusion, Thyer states that "twenty years ago the field of behavioral social work could not be said to exist. It is now well established and growing, with the potential to become the dominant school of practice" (p. 134).

In his 1983 presidential address to the Association for Advancement of Behavior Therapy, K. D. O'Leary summarized by saying, "Behavior therapy has become one of the major theoretical orientations of psychologists treating children and adults. With children, the orientation is a major one; with adults it is one of the top two orientations, about on an equal par with a psychodynamic orientation. Our influence has been felt in the treatment journals of psychologists, psychiatrists, and social workers. . . . Our influence in the treatment research arena probably is the area of our greatest impact. Behavioral research projects constitute approximately 70% of the psychosocial treatment research funded by the U.S. National Institute of Mental Health. Our image in newspapers, as reflected in *The New York Times,* has become more positive in the past few years. . . . When clients or patients receive our services, generally they view us very positively. We have developed treatments for a number of serious problems for children and adults, and it is time for us to work together with other professionals and inform the public of our progress" (O'Leary, 1984, p. 230).

In this book, I intend to provide the student with an understanding of the history and theoretical underpinnings of behavior modification, to teach some of the specific procedures and techniques used by therapists, to show the breadth of application of those procedures, and, in general, to give an appreciation for the behavioral approach to clinical psychology.

Chapter

1

Historical Overview: The Origins of Behavior Modification

Craighead, Kazdin, and Mahoney (1981) state the interesting and provocative position that "the history of behavior modification is as old as the history of human beings" (p. 6). By this they mean that the basic principles of both operant and classical learning theory did not wait for their systematization in the twentieth century to exert their influence over human and animal behavior, any more than gravity waited for Sir Isaac Newton in the eighteenth century to exert its pull.

EARLY HISTORY

Kazdin (1978) provides numerous historical examples and illustrations of what today would be called operant conditioning, contingency management, or behavior modification. He describes the delivery of rewards (wreaths, crowns, feathers, money, property, statues, privilege, and freedom) for triumphant military performances by first-century Greek and Roman gladiators and charioteers, fifteenth-century Aztec soldiers, and pre-Columbian American Plains Indians. He further describes the use of prizes such as nuts, figs, cakes, and honey as rewards for students who were studying Greek and Latin and learning to recite their lessons in twelfth- and sixteenth-century European schools.

   Both Kazdin (1978) and Pitts (1976) describe the reward system used in a British penal colony on Norfolk Island, Australia, in the nineteenth century. The "primary basis of rehabilitation was a 'mark system' in which sentences were converted into a fixed number of 'marks' that individuals had to earn to obtain release. . . . The main treatment consisted of inmates earning marks for work and for appropriate conduct. The marks could be exchanged for essential items, including food, shelter, and clothes. Disciplinary offenses were punished by fines and by withdrawal of privileges rather than by the cruel measures that had been commonly practiced (e.g., flogging and being bound in chains)" (Kazdin, 1978, p. 238). This mark system will later be referred to as a "token economy."

In addition, Krueger (1961) describes the cruel and aversive punishment conditioning procedure employed by a Chinese emperor's son while commanding his troops in 200 B.C., and Snortum (1976) reviews Benjamin Franklin's eighteenth-century, 13-week course of behavioral self-monitoring aimed at increasing the frequency of 13 virtues. Clearly, "long before the principles of operant conditioning were investigated explicitly, various behavior-change techniques were used that bear similarity to contemporary operant techniques. The techniques, of course, were not conceived of as operant conditioning and, indeed, preceded the formal development of psychology itself" (Kazdin, 1978, p. 234).

MODERN TIMES

Although Craighead, Kazdin, and Mahoney (1981) claim behavior modification to be as old as history, they note that "the study of the systematic application of behavior modification is a comparatively new endeavor" (p. 6). They and others (e.g., Martin & Pear, 1983; Rimm & Masters, 1979) give credit predominantly to two twentieth-century Americans whose research and writings most influenced the development and growth of the field.

Watson

The first is John B. Watson (1878–1958), frequently referred to as the "father of behaviorism." In his famous 1913 paper, "Psychology as the Behaviorist Views It," and his 1924 book, *Behaviorism,* he presented his position that psychology should no longer consider consciousness as its primary domain of study. Instead, he argued, one need be concerned only with objective, measurable, observable, overt behavior, and that behavior is merely a series of learned habits, following certain rules and controlled by the environment. Although academic and research interest in behaviorism gradually and steadily grew during the early decades of this century, relatively few articles reported the *clinical* applications of these principles.

Skinner

The great proliferation of studies illustrating the applicability of behavioral principles to the treatment of human clinical problems is mainly attributed to the second major influence in the field—B. F. Skinner (b. 1904). In his 1938 book, *The Behavior of Organisms,* based on his research with rats, he outlined what have become the basic tenets of operant conditioning. In the journal articles that followed, these tenets were extended to the control of human behavior. An example of a frequently cited and typical early report is that by Fuller (1949), who showed that a profoundly retarded, bedridden, institutionalized patient (described as a "vegetative idiot" and thought not to have learned anything in his 18 years of life) could be taught to raise his arm to a vertical position within four experimental sessions when a sugar and milk solution was injected into his mouth as the reward. This was one of the earliest attempts to use operant conditioning in a clinical setting with a human.

Peters (1952, 1955) applied basic operant conditioning procedures to a group of 36 "extremely withdrawn schizophrenics of poor prognosis" (1952, p. 354). Each of these patients had to meet three requirements to be included in the study: They already had to have been in the hospital for more than a year; all other treatments, including electroshock, must have failed; and no other therapeutic program could have been planned. In other words, these were the hard-core, back-ward schizophrenic patients. The subjects were all made hungry (food deprived by delayed breakfast) and divided into an experimental group and two control groups. As part of their 12-week occupational therapy (O.T.) program, the experimental group spent the first 6 weeks working with a variety of multiple-trial problem-solving tasks such as mazes, discrimination problems, and multiple-choice boxes. They were rewarded with bite-sized pieces of fudge for their active participation. "The results show that the problem solving group increased in work performance during the second half of the treatment period, while the other groups actually decreased in performance. Assuming that work performance under the conditions which were present is an indicator of a patient's mental condition, it can be concluded that the intensive problem solving was a favorable factor" (1955, p. 188).

In his 1953 book, *Science and Human Behavior,* Skinner extended the influence of operant conditioning beyond animals and the most severely disturbed humans. He elaborated and expanded on his own earlier thinking to show how operant principles influence the behavior of people in virtually all aspects of their lives, including government and law, economics, education, and even religion. The foundation had thus been laid.

The next several decades reflected the rapid rise of behavior modification to its current status. "The growth of the field has been nothing short of phenomenal" (Rimm & Masters, 1979, p. 4). Bijou and Baer (1961) were the first to conceptualize child development in operant terms, and the first major book of readings was Ullman and Krasner's (1965) *Case Studies in Behavior Modification,* probably the first book with "behavior modification" in its title. The Association for Advancement of Behavior Therapy (AABT) was founded in 1966, followed by the publication of numerous journals, such as the *Journal of Applied Behavior Analysis* in 1968 and *Behavior Therapy* in 1970. "In less than 20 years, it has brought about a major reconceptualization of psychological problems and their treatment" (Kazdin, 1978, p. ix).

Chapter
2

Theoretical Overview: The Principles of Operant Conditioning

The theoretical underpinnings of behavior modification and contingency management are the principles of operant conditioning. These principles have their historical origins in the works of E. L. Thorndike (1911) and B. F. Skinner (1938, 1953).

Operant conditioning can be defined as a system of behavior change based on an alteration of the consequences of an action. That is, a behavior can be made to increase or decrease in some observable and quantifiable way (e.g., probability, frequency, duration, or intensity of occurrence) depending on the consequences of that behavior. A consequence is considered to be contingent when it occurs only as a result of the behavior preceding it. Walker and Shea (1980, p. 21), referring to Sarason, Glaser, and Fargo (1972), colloquially describe this operant paradigm as "What you do is influenced by what follows what you do." Tennov (1975) succinctly refers to this as the "3 R's rule": *r*einforced *r*esponses *r*ecur. Quite simply put, a child praised by his or her teacher for answering a question may be more likely to speak up in the future; a child ridiculed by his or her classmates for an incorrect answer may be less likely to speak up again.

Thorndike's (1911) theory of learning includes his "Law of Effect," one of the historical cornerstones of operant conditioning. Although he subsequently revised portions of it (to decrease the importance and effectiveness of punishment), the Law of Effect, in part, states, "Of several responses made to the same situation, those which are accompanied or closely followed by satisfaction to the animal will, other things being equal, be more firmly connected with the situation, so that, when it recurs, they will be more likely to recur; those which are accompanied or closely followed by discomfort to the animal will, other things being equal, have their connections with that situation weakened, so that, when it recurs, they will be less likely to occur" (p. 244).

Skinner (1953) uses the term *operant* to mean a class of responses and emphasizes the fact that "the behavior operates upon the environment to generate consequences" (p. 65). In operant conditioning, he states, one "strengthens an operant in the sense of making a response more probable or, in actual fact, more frequent" (p. 65). The classical illustration of Skinner's principles is that of the operant conditioning chamber (or the so-called "Skinner Box"). Here, for example, a rat presses a lever (the operant response) and receives, contingent on that response, a few pellets of food (the consequence). Assuming the desirability of the food and following the Law of Effect, the rate of the rat's lever pressing should increase. This is operant conditioning.

With behavior modification or contingency management defined as the therapeutic and systematic manipulation of operant conditioning (i.e., of contingent behavioral consequences), these consequences fall into one of four mutually exclusive (but not necessarily exhaustive) categories: positive reinforcement, negative reinforcement, positive punishment, and negative punishment. Table 2.1 (adapted from Craighead, Kazdin, & Mahoney, 1981, p. 116; Kanfer & Phillips, 1970, p. 253; Olton & Noonberg, 1980, p. 25; Tryon, 1976, p. 510; and Woods, 1974, p. 585) illustrates these relationships and also provides a variety of synonymous descriptive terms. For reference, each box is numbered, and the incremental or decremental effect it has on behavior is designated by the direction of the arrow in the lower right corner.

POSITIVE REINFORCEMENT

Positive reinforcement as a procedure or process (box 1) refers to the increase of some prescribed measure of a behavior (e.g., frequency) resulting from the behavior-positive reinforcer contingency. That is, *the administration of a positive reinforcer as the contingent consequence of a behavior* increases the frequency of that behavior as indicated by the upward direction of the arrow. The previously described study by Fuller (1949)—teaching an arm-raising response to a retarded patient with a sugar and milk solution as the positive reinforcer—illustrates the principle of positive reinforcement. Another illustration is the study by Bacon-Prue, Blount, Hosey, and Drabman (1980), who followed bed-making behavior in a group of males at a residential facility for the retarded by posting their photographs on a "bedmakers" poster board. The percentage of beds made in their study rose from a mean of 21 percent during baseline to a mean of 64 percent during the positive reinforcement phase.

Carney, Schechter, and Davis (1983) increased adherence to a necessary medical regimen—blood glucose testing—in a group of insulin-dependent diabetic children. As can be seen from Figure 2.1, the treatment

Table 2.1 MANIPULATION OF CONTINGENT CONSEQUENCES

Contingent Stimulus Event	Operation Performed on Stimulus Event	
	Onset of . . . **Increase of . . .** **Administration/application of . . .**	**Offset of . . .** **Decrease of . . .** **Withdrawal/removal of . . .**
Positive reinforcer **Appetitive stimulus** **"Pleasant" stimulus** **Reward**	1. *Positive reinforcement* Reward conditioning	3. *Negative punishment* Response cost Penalty conditioning Punishment by removal
Negative reinforcer **Aversive stimulus** **"Unpleasant" stimulus** **Punisher**	2. *Positive punishment* Punishment by application Punishment conditioning	4. *Negative reinforcement* Relief conditioning Escape

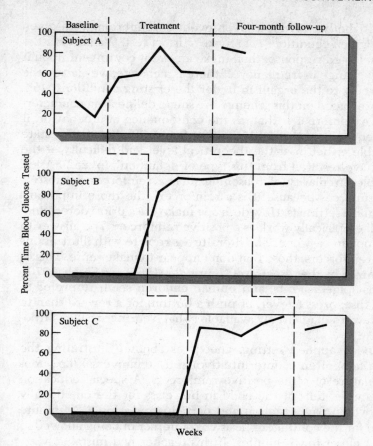

Figure 2.1 The percentage of time blood glucose was tested each week for the three subjects during baseline, treatment, and follow-up. (*Source:* R. N. Carney, K. Schechter, & T. Davis, Improving adherence to blood glucose testing in insulin-dependent children, *Behavior Therapy, 14* (1983), 247–254. Copyright 1983 by the Association for Advancement of Behavior Therapy. Reprinted by permission of the publisher and the authors.)

condition produced a dramatic and stable improvement in the percentage of times the children tested their blood. Treatment consisted of a combination of contingent praise and the awarding of points for the completion of the blood-monitoring procedure—the reinforcement. Clearly, positive reinforcement increased behavior.

What Is a Reinforcer?

A major question that should arise at this point is, What exactly is a positive reinforcer? On a purely empirical basis, Skinner (1953) says, "the only defining characteristic of a reinforcing stimulus is that it reinforces. The only way to tell whether or not a given event is reinforcing to a given organism under given conditions is to make a direct test. We observe the frequency of a selected response, then make an event contingent upon it and observe any change in frequency. If there is a change, we classify the event as reinforcing to the organism under the existing conditions" (pp. 72–73). Therefore, based on this schema, the single delineating characteristic of a positive reinforcer is that, as the consequence of a behavior, it increases the frequency of that behavior. Kanfer and Phillips (1970) state that "considerable criticism at the theoretical level and difficulty at the practical level have resulted from this type of definition" (p. 252). Aside from the possible circularity of reasoning (it is a reinforcer because it reinforces; it reinforces because it is a reinforcer), the more important question in a clinical setting is, How does one make the a priori determination of what will empirically work as a positive reinforcer? The answer to this question is not an easy one. The literature is replete with illustrations of nonintuitive reinforcers, those that don't appear to make sense. This is, perhaps, epitomized by the research of Neuringer (1969) and Singh (1970), who showed that pigeons, rats, and human children seem to prefer to "work" (peck a disc, press a lever, or push a button) for a reward than to have the same reward made freely available (what Neuringer called "free-loading").

Similarly, in an applied setting, anecdotes abound illustrating the nonintuitive (in fact, often counterintuitive) and nonuniversal (i.e., non-generalizable) nature of some positive reinforcers. A special education teacher, for example, tells of the child in her class for the emotionally disturbed who would pay attention and participate during a 30-minute academic lesson for the contingent positive reinforcer of being allowed to go into the coat closet for 5 minutes. If this teacher had mistakenly accepted the universality of this positive reinforcer, and placed each child into the closet as a technique for increasing academic behaviors, she surely would have eventually found a child for whom this consequence would certainly have been anything but positive reinforcement.

How, then, does the practitioner choose a positive reinforcer if, according to Gambrill (1977), each of us has a unique "reinforcer profile"? Although Rimm and Masters (1979) state that one of the "fundamental defining characteristics" of behavior therapy is the great value placed on obtaining empirical support for the various techniques employed and that, therefore, the development of a reinforcer is not an intuitive process, Gambrill provides several strategies for deductive reasoning in order to "locate" positive reinforcers. These include observing the client's behavior, examining deprivation states, asking significant others, and asking the client orally or with written schedules. For example, Cautela (1977, 1981) provides numerous reinforcement survey schedules, each developed for a different population (e.g., adults, children in kindergarten through third grade, children in fourth through sixth grade, adolescents, autistic children, the visually impaired, adults in hospital settings, and the elderly).

These psychometric devices can provide the practitioner with at least some clues concerning what would be a positive reinforcer for a particular client.

Wacker, Berg, Wiggins, Muldoon, and Cavanaugh (1985) describe the particular difficulties involved in determining appropriate reinforcers for the physically handicapped: "The limited response repertoires of students with profound/multiple handicaps often result in unreliable assumptions regarding the students' preferences toward various stimuli. A major need for these students is to develop systematic procedures for evaluating potential reinforcers" (p. 173). Using a system of microswitches that could be activated by very small or subtle motor movements of the arm or head, the researchers allowed even subjects suffering from cerebral palsy or spastic quadriplegia to choose from among several potential reinforcers.

Primary Reinforcers

Part of the potential confusion over the definition of a reinforcer may arise from the fact that positive reinforcers fall into at least five categories. The first are called **primary** or **unconditioned reinforcers**. "These are reinforcing stimuli that are not dependent on the individual's past history of conditioning and are encountered in most members of a species. Food, water, stimuli that reduce discomfort or pain, and sexual stimuli are among those that are generally attractive to most people at most times" (Kanfer & Phillips, 1970, pp. 255–256). Primary reinforcers exert their influence on behavior because their desirable characteristics are inherent in their nature and appear to best fit Hull's (1943) drive-reduction model of motivation and reinforcement. This explains why food deprivation and the proverbial M & M candies are so popular.

Conditioned Reinforcers

The second type are called **conditioned** or **secondary** or **generalized reinforcers**. These are often originally neutral stimuli that have gained reinforcing properties through a contiguous learning relationship with a primary reinforcer. They are, as well, often "cashed in" for a primary reinforcer. Money, tokens, points, stars, checkmarks, stamps, stickers, and happy faces are common examples of this type of reinforcer. The points given to the children by Carney, Schechter, and Davis (1983) for completing their blood glucose testing are conditioned reinforcers.

Social Reinforcers

The third type, **social reinforcers**, tend to straddle the line between primary and secondary reinforcers. Verbal praise—as with all language—has to be learned and is, therefore, a conditioned reinforcer, whereas physical contact (e.g., hugging) is probably an unconditioned reinforcer (contact need) (Harlow, 1958).

Sensory Reinforcers

In addition to the more obvious and common "external" reinforcers (e.g., food, objects), Kish (1966) developed a theory revolving around **sensory reinforcement**—the "reinforcing effects of the sensory consequences of behavior" itself (p. 110). This fourth type of reinforcement could include visual and auditory exploration, gustation, manipulation, touch, and stimulus change. Kish states that "the sensory reinforcement hypothesis postulates that response-contingent stimulation in any modality is reinforcing" and that these sensory reinforcers are unrelated to the usual organic drive state (p. 148). Rincover and Newsom (1985) use a sensory-reinforcement model to explain much of the self-stimulatory behaviors seen in an autistic population. These individuals are frequently observed clapping hands, tapping fingers, stroking hair, and rubbing cloth. It is known that they "do not typically show preferences for social events, such as smiles, praise, gestures, or the closeness of others" (p. 237). On the other hand, "the implication may be that sensory stimulation is a powerful and durable class of reinforcers" for this population (p. 237).

The Premack Principle

Somewhat more unusual, the fifth type conceives of a positive reinforcer not as an object or thing given to a subject but as a response or behavior or activity that the subject is allowed (has the opportunity) to engage in. As conceptualized by David Premack (1962), responses of low probability can be reinforced (i.e., made more probable) if responses of high probability are made contingent on them. That is, a high-probability response (e.g., watching television or eating dessert) will reinforce a low-probability response (e.g., doing homework or eating vegetables) and make it more probable.

Following an initial assessment of behavior and the development of a response-probability hierarchy, Homme, deBaca, Devine, Steinhorst, and Rickert (1963) applied the so-called **Premack principle** to a class of nursery school children. The low-probability response of sitting quietly in a chair and looking at the blackboard was intermittently reinforced by the opportunity to leap to one's feet and run around the room screaming (high-probability response). The researchers report that "with this kind of procedure, control was virtually perfect after a few days" (p. 544).

Martin and Pear (1983) also divided positive reinforcers into five categories and used the acronym C-A-M-P-S to stand for consumables, activities, manipulatives, possessionals, and social reinforcers. Examples of each would include, respectively, candy and other food; watching television;

working on puzzles; receiving trinkets; and smiles, hugs, and verbalizations.

Schedules of Reinforcement

Whatever positive reinforcer is finally decided on, it can be presented to the client on one or more of a large number of **schedules of reinforcement**. "The schedule of reinforcement is the rule followed . . . in determining which among the many occurrences of a response will be reinforced" (Reynolds, 1968, pp. 59–60). A positive reinforcer can either follow every response emission (**continuous reinforcement**, CRF) or follow on an **intermittent** or **partial reinforcement** schedule. "Under intermittent reinforcement, only selected occurrences of a response are reinforced" (p. 59). Intermittent schedules can be divided into two main classifications. **Ratio** (or frequency) **schedules** require a specified number of responses to be emitted before contingent reinforcement is presented. **Interval** (or temporal) **schedules** require a specified time interval since the previous presentation of the reinforcement must elapse before a response will be reinforced. "Under ratio schedules the amount of time the organism takes to emit the necessary number of responses is irrelevant, while under interval schedules the number of responses is irrelevant so long as the organism emits the one response necessary for reinforcement after the interval has elapsed" (p. 60).

Ratio and interval intermittent schedules can be further subdivided into two classifications. In **fixed ratio** (FR) schedules, reinforcement occurs every time a set number of responses is emitted. The number of responses required is the same for each presentation of the reinforcement; that is, it is "fixed." In a **variable ratio** (VR) schedule, reinforcement is again contingent on a certain number of responses being emitted, but this number is variable; that is, it changes from reinforcement to reinforcement. In a **fixed interval** (FI) schedule, the first response after a set period of time has elapsed will be reinforced. This time interval is fixed or consistent from reinforcement to reinforcement. In contrast, this interval is varied for each reinforcement in a **variable interval** (VI) schedule.

The practical importance of these different schedules is that "each schedule of reinforcement produces a characteristic performance. Depending on the schedule involved, the performance may consist of a steady, predictable rate of responding or of regular, oscillating, and predictable changes in rate" (Reynolds, 1968, pp. 61–62). A continuous reinforcement schedule usually produces faster acquisition of a learned response, but partial schedules usually produce more stable response rates, fewer administrations of reinforcement, and greater subsequent resistance to extinction if or when reinforcement is discontinued. In a clinical setting, these schedule-induced effects (especially resistance to extinction) often prove to be of great practical importance in the control of the behavior under question. This topic will be discussed further in Chapters 6 and 7.

POSITIVE PUNISHMENT

The corollary of positive reinforcement as the administration of a positive reinforcer is **positive punishment** (box 2), *the administration of a negative reinforcer* (also known as a punishing, aversive, or "unpleasant" stimulus) *as the contingent consequence of a behavior.* In a rephrasing of Skinner's empirical definition of a reinforcer, Azrin and Holz (1966) define a negative reinforcer as "a consequence of behavior that reduces the future probability of that behavior" (p. 381). This suppression of behavior is indicated by the downward direction of the arrow in box 2 of Table 2.1. By way of comparison, Thorndike, as part of his 1911 learning theory, spoke of positive and negative reinforcers as "satisfiers" and "annoyers." "By a satisfying state of affairs is meant one which the animal does nothing to avoid, often doing such things as attain and preserve it. By a discomforting or annoying state of affairs is meant one which the animal commonly avoids and abandons" (p. 245).

What Is an Aversive Stimulus?

Although on an intuitive level one seems to understand what an aversive stimulus is, the same problems arise as with positive reinforcers. Things are not always as they seem, and intuition occasionally falters. This is quite nicely illustrated in a study by Madsen, Becker, Thomas, Koser, and Plager (1970), referred to by Craighead, Kazdin, and Mahoney (1981). In classrooms of first-grade children, teachers verbally reprimanded (presumably a negative reinforcer) students for inappropriate out-of-seat behavior in an attempt to reduce the frequency of this disruptive response. However, the results indicated a positive correlation between the frequency of reprimands and the frequency of subsequent out-of-seat behavior. That is, the more the teachers reprimanded, the more the children stood. The interpretation of this counterintuitive finding is based on the empirical data— what was initially thought to be a negative reinforcer turned out to be, instead, a positive reinforcer.

Positive punishment is quite clearly illustrated in a study by Singh, Dawson, and Gregory (1980) in which "response-contingent aromatic ammonia as the aversive stimulus was used to suppress chronic hyperventilation in a 17.5 year-old profoundly retarded female" (p. 561). When a vial of ammonia was held under her nose for three seconds each time she hyperventilated (often associated with impaired consciousness, palpitations, and convulsions), the frequency of this behavior dropped from a mean of approximately 8.7 per minute during baseline observation to a rate of close to zero during subsequent observation periods. It should be noted here that although the procedure involved the administration of an aversive (albeit, harmless) stimulus, it was apparently justified by the medical complications of the problem behavior. Ethical concerns are discussed further in Chapter 7.

Analogous to primary and conditioned positive reinforcers, a **primary negative reinforcer** (e.g., ammonia, electric shock, loud noise) does not depend on one's past learning history for its aversiveness. A **conditioned negative reinforcer**, on the other hand, does; that is, it is an originally neutral stimulus that has become aversive because of its pairing with a primary negative reinforcer. This also includes such social stimuli as the verbalization "No, that's bad!"

NEGATIVE PUNISHMENT

If positive and negative reinforcers can be administered as the contingent consequence of behavior, they can also be withdrawn. This constitutes the second half of Table 2.1 (boxes 3 and 4). The withdrawal of a positive reinforcer contingent on the emission of a response is called **negative punishment** or *response cost* or *penalty conditioning*. The effect is to suppress the likelihood of a behavior (note the downward arrow).

Forman (1980) developed a response-cost program that *fined* elementary school children who had been referred to the school psychologist for aggressive behavior. Each such incident led to a 2-minute deduction from a twice-weekly 30-minute session during which the children could play ball or listen to music and dance. That is, the procedure was to withdraw a positive reinforcer—something the children wanted—contingent on an exhibition of aggression. Results showed a significant reduction in each of the five dependent measures of aggression used.

NEGATIVE REINFORCEMENT

The withdrawal of a negative reinforcer as the consequence of a behavior is called **negative reinforcement** (box 4), and its effect is to increase the emission of that behavior (up-turned arrow). Milberg and Hebben (1979) successfully treated a 77-year-old anorexic male, who vehemently denied being an uncooperative patient, by giving him the choice between eating at least half the food given to him or engaging in a complex and time-consuming self-monitoring program. The results indicated that he chose to eat in order to *escape* from the record keeping. In a very similar study, Kazdin and Mascitelli (1980), in part using a token reward system, improved attentive classroom behavior in two retarded children by providing them with the opportunity to earn their way off the system. Lovitt and Hansen (1976) improved both oral reading rates and comprehension scores in a group of learning-disabled children. The intervention involved allowing the students to skip all the remaining assigned material in that section of the book if their scores equaled or exceeded the criterion set for that day. The results of these three studies seem to indicate that under certain circumstances, data collection, token reward systems, and reading material can all be viewed as aversive stimuli!

IN REVIEW

In reviewing the four boxes in Table 2.1, it can be noted that both boxes called "reinforcement" (1 and 4) increase behavior, whereas both boxes called "punishment" (2 and 3) decrease behavior. Additionally, both boxes called "positive" (1 and 2) involve the administration of a stimulus event, whereas both boxes called "negative" (3 and 4) involve the withdrawal of a stimulus event.

Interestingly, to utilize negative punishment, a positive reinforcer must first be presented in order to be subsequently withdrawn. Could the presentation of this positive reinforcer be inadvertent positive reinforcement? Similarly, a negative reinforcer sets the stage for negative reinforcement; that is, a negative reinforcer must first be presented in order to be later withdrawn. Could its presentation be interpreted as unintentional positive punishment? Think about it.

The four boxes of Table 2.1 involve the contingent consequences following the *emission* of a response. Woods (1974) and Tryon (1976) double the number of boxes in the table to eight by considering and including the consequences of the *omission* of a response. In other words, a positive reinforcer can be administered (positive reinforcement) not only as the consequence of making a given response (emission) but also as the consequence of not making that response (omission). The same holds true for the other three relationships. Omission training, as more than merely semantics, forms the basis of a very important intervention strategy—DRO—to be discussed in Chapter 4.

Chapter
3

Treatment Overview: Goals and Diagnoses

In 1973, D. L. Rosenhan's article, "On Being Sane in Insane Places," made an important point for those involved in clinical work. Rosenhan had eight "sane" people secretly institutionalized in various psychiatric hospitals by claiming to hear hallucinated voices. On the basis of these supposed hallucinations, each was admitted and diagnosed as schizophrenic. Although once admitted to the hospital these "patients" made every attempt to act "normally" (i.e., "sane"), much of their subsequent behavior was interpreted in light of their psychotic diagnosis. For example, writing (note taking for Rosenhan) was viewed as an aspect of pathological behavior, pacing the halls (boredom) was interpreted as nervousness, and sitting outside the cafeteria one-half hour before it opened was interpreted as the oral-acquisitive nature of the psychotic syndrome.

The point is that once given a psychiatric label, a patient's future behavior is often viewed and interpreted in the context of that label. The circularity of this process should be apparent: The original diagnostic label is based on certain behavioral aberrations, and future behavior is then interpreted, not in and of itself, but on the basis of that label. In such a system, how can patients ever show themselves to be sane? In Rosenhan's example, they couldn't. None of the "pseudopatients" was ever detected by the hospital staff, although 35 of the 118 patients on the ward voiced their suspicions. When they were discharged (a writ of habeas corpus was prepared for each pseudopatient as a precaution), the discharge diagnosis was "schizophrenic in remission."

DSM–III DIAGNOSES

Most traditional diagnostic systems like the American Psychiatric Association's *Diagnostic and Statistical Manual of Mental Disorders* (*DSM*–III, 1979; *DSM*–III-R, 1987) assess a patient's behavior and then assign a particular categorical label and number to it. Several problems arise from this practice. Aside from the previously discussed problem of "once labeled, always viewed," such diagnostic systems often engender a certain amount of dissatisfaction (see Kazdin, 1978) on the more basic questions of validity and reliability. That is, questions arise regarding the strength of the relationship between assessed behavior and diagnostic nomenclature and the extent to which different diagnoses are reliably differentiated. Zubin (1967), in reviewing the literature, felt that overall agreement among different observers was, perhaps, too low to be clinically useful.

Morris and Kratochwill (1983) criticize any categorical or typology approach to diagnosis because of the problems inherent in treating psychiatric conditions as separate and distinct entities. They refer to Begelman (1976), who discusses at least nine criticisms of the *DSM* system, including (1) facilitating the stigmatization of the individual, (2) excessive reliance on the medical model of abnormal behavior, (3) poor or low reliability and validity, and, quite important, (4) little relevance toward treatment plans (pp. 23–24).

In perhaps the most stinging criticism of *DSM*–III, McReynolds (1979) complains that "it provides a restrictive framework for the growth and application of psychological knowledge. The incipient new order extends current psychiatric thinking by encompassing scores of new behavioral disturbances within the 'medical model' and by defining mental disorders circumstantially in terms of psychiatric practice. Although extensive nosological statements of the manner and form of behavioral disturbance appear to be appropriate for medical science, such categorical representations of behavioral processes are no longer defensible in social science" (p. 123). On the value of the medical model or disease entity conception of categorical behavioral disturbances, McReynolds concludes, "That well is dry" (p. 125). Quay, Routh, and Shapiro (1987), in reviewing the origins of traditional diagnostic labeling, note, "Taxonomies of psychopathology historically have been derived by means of the observations of clinicians working with disordered individuals. Since most of these clinicians were physicians, it was natural that they followed the traditional methods of clinical medicine in attempting to describe symptoms . . . and to decipher the underlying disorders" (p. 492).

It should be apparent that what is now clearly needed is a new, *behavioral* approach to diagnosis.

BEHAVIORAL DIAGNOSIS

A **behavioral diagnostic system** is one that focuses exclusively on patients' behavior itself, that is, what the patients *do,* not what they *are.* As an advantage of focusing only on behavior, one avoids the circularity of the behavior-label-behavior tautology ("Johnny is aggressive because he hits other children; he hits other children because he is aggressive"). A behavioral system would simply state, "Johnny hits other children." This approach is usually followed in marital therapy, where couples are counseled not to call each other names ("You're such a slob!") but to focus on the undesirable behavior ("You always throw your dirty clothes on the floor!").

Instead of choosing from as many as several hundred traditional diagnostic categories (in fact, *DSM*–III, 1979, shows a 60 percent increase in the total number of psychiatric disorders as compared to *DSM*–II, 1968, and a 280 percent increase as compared to *DSM*–I, 1952), a system focusing on behavior can have as few as *three.* If behavior is viewed in terms of its observable components—frequency, duration, intensity, setting—maladaptive behavior can be viewed as falling into one of these three categories: *behavioral deficit* (engaging in some behavior too infrequently, for too short a duration, or with insufficient intensity), *behavioral excess* (engaging in some behavior too frequently, for too long a duration, or with too much intensity), or *behavioral inappropriateness* (a stimulus-control problem involving what could be an appropriate behavior but at an inappropriate place or time, i.e., setting).

Deficit-Excess Continuum

One can frequently view behavioral deficiencies and excesses as opposite ends of a continuum (see Table 3.1) with "normal, adaptive behavior" (in terms of frequency, duration, etc.) falling somewhere in between. Of

Table 3.1   BEHAVIORAL DIAGNOSTIC CONTINUUM

Behavioral Deficit ← Normal → Behavioral Excess	
Frequency-Duration-Intensity Continuum	
Examples	Examples
Anorexia	Delusional speech
Adherence to medical regimen	Out-of-seat behavior
Seat belt usage	Bed-wetting
Punctuality	Aggression
Task performance	Hyperventilation
In-seat studying	Smoking
Physical exercise	Self-injurious behavior

course, this schema is not universally correct; some behaviors can be viewed as excessive with a frequency of only once (e.g., murder). However, using the deficiency-excess continuum as a model, one can see that a deficiency of one behavior could be interpreted as an excess of some opposite, incompatible behavior and vice versa. For example, a student who frequently leaves his seat and disturbs others in class during a lesson clearly manifests an excess of "out-of-seat" behavior. Equally, however, this could be viewed as a deficit of "in-seat and attending" behavior. More than merely a semantic exercise, this model proves quite useful as the basis of a therapeutic technique (DRO), as will be seen in Chapter 4.

These diagnostic categories, in addition to their parsimony and brevity, have the additional advantage of being *prescriptive*. Once a maladaptive behavior is placed into its appropriate category, *treatment goals* immediately become clear. Simply stated, *behavioral deficits are to be increased* and *behavioral excesses decreased* toward the more adaptive "middle ground." This text presents various intervention strategies specifically aimed at accomplishing these goals. A number of other books (e.g., Axelrod, 1977; Berni & Fordyce, 1977; Martin & Pear, 1983; Ross, 1981; and Walker & Shea, 1980) also arrange their contents around this prescriptive approach.

This deficit-excess diagnostic system, with its explicit treatment goal, has found application both inside and outside traditional clinical settings. As an illustration, Rimm and Masters (1979) provide a table (Table 6.1, pp. 214–217) with more than 70 target behavior problems for which behavior modification has demonstrated effectiveness. These behavior problems fall into such categories as contingency management of psychological and emotional problems: gender identity, hyperactivity, psychosomatic disorders, anxiety, depression, and pain; contingency management in education: maximizing academic performance, teaching academic skills, and controlling disruptive behaviors; and contingency management with the retarded, with the delinquent, with a prison population, and with institutionalized psychotics.

If operant conditioning and contingency management are viewed in the broadest sense as techniques or procedures to alter the likelihood (increase or decrease) of a given behavior or behaviors, the litany of such behaviors and, therefore, the applicability of these procedures are limited only by one's imagination. A review of the literature clearly illustrates this point.

Illustrations from the Published Literature

In an institutional setting, Foxx, McMorrow, Bittle, and Bechtel (1986) reduced the incidence of severe self-injurious behaviors (behavioral excesses) by using a punishment procedure. Davis, Wallace, Liberman, and Finch (1976) utilized a milder aversive procedure (time-out) in an attempt to suppress delusional and hallucinatory speech (behavioral excess), and

Vingoe (1980) reduced the frequency of obsessive-compulsive ritualistic behaviors (excesses). Halmi, Powers, and Cunningham (1975) made a variety of social reinforcers contingent on weight gain in a case of anorexia nervosa, characterized by refusal to eat (behavioral deficit). Burgio, Page, and Capriotti (1985) reduced the incidence of aggressive, disruptive, and self-stimulatory behaviors (all behavioral excesses) in a group of severely and profoundly mentally retarded individuals while at the same time increasing in-seat, attending behaviors (behavioral deficits).

With a twist of who is considered the "patient," Hollander and Plutchik (1972) increased the percentage of assigned tasks performed (behavioral deficit) by a group of psychiatric *attendants* with contingent trading stamps, redeemable in local stores for merchandise. In a medical hospital, Baile and Engel (1978) developed a program based, in part, on contingent reinforcement and designed to increase treatment compliance (behavioral deficit) by patients following myocardial infarction; and Patterson and Jackson (1980), working with an elderly population, increased food consumption, self-feeding, ambulation, and exercise (all behavioral deficits) with a variety of contingent reinforcers. McCaul, Stitzer, Bigelow, and Liebson (1984) developed a reward program to increase the percentage of opiate-free urines (behavioral deficit) in a group of former heroin addicts on methadone maintenance.

Using both social reinforcement contingent on appropriate quiet work (behavioral deficit) and aversive social consequences for inappropriate talking (behavioral excess), McAllister, Stachowiak, Baer, and Conderman (1969) applied contingency management successfully in a secondary school classroom.

In an industrial setting, Hermann, deMontes, Dominquez, Montes, and Hopkins (1973) reduced the tardiness of workers (behavioral excess) by reinforcing punctuality (behavioral deficit) with cash bonuses; Bourdon (1977) described a contingency management program involving both tangible (catalog items) and intangible (social) reinforcers to alter efficiency, quality, attendance (all behavioral deficits) and waste (behavioral excess) in a large corporation; and Quilitch (1978) increased the submission of written suggestions (behavioral deficit).

In a community setting, Clark, Burgess, and Hendee (1972) reduced the amount of littering (behavioral excess) in a national forest campground by rewarding children—for example, with inexpensive shoulder patches—for collecting trash; Everett, Hayward, and Meyer (1974) increased bus ridership (behavioral deficit) by over 150 percent through the use of token reinforcement; Meyers, Nathan, and Kopel (1977) found the same procedure effective in increasing the frequency of journal reshelving (behavioral deficit) in a college library; and Roberts and Fanurik (1986) boosted seat-belt usage (behavioral deficit) from 4.3 percent to 66.2 percent with positive reinforcement.

In the setting of the home, Azrin and Foxx (1974) and Azrin and Thienes (1978) presented a variety of procedures to control childhood enuresis (behavioral excess); Clark, Greene, Macrae, McNees, Davis, and Risley (1977) developed a "parent advice package" aimed at reducing children's disruptive behaviors (behavioral excess) and increasing appropriate social and verbal behaviors (behavioral deficit) while on shopping trips; Heller and Strang (1973) reduced the incidence of bruxism (behavioral excess) with aversive consequences in a 24-year-old male who had been grinding his teeth almost nightly; Blount, Baer, and Collins (1984) increased adherence to visual training exercises (behavioral deficit) in an 11-year-old boy; Jason (1984) decreased excessive TV viewing while increasing school-, play-, and housework-related activities (behavioral deficits); and Hobbs, Walle, and Caldwell (1984) reduced various conduct problems such as noncompliance.

Once again, as all these examples illustrate, the diagnosis is both behaviorally descriptive and prescriptive, and the treatment goal is clear.

Chapter
4

The Interventions

Behavior modification or contingency management provides a *series* of procedures and techniques aimed at remediating target behavioral deficits and excesses. The term *series* was chosen over another term, *compilation,* because of its specific connotation. Rimm and Masters (1979) state, as one of the cornerstones of behavior therapy, that the behavior therapist "adapts his method of treatment to the client's problem" (p. 10). Therefore, rather than randomly or haphazardly choosing one of perhaps a half-dozen or more procedures to employ, a therapist should view a contingency management intervention strategy as a systematic and stepwise progression, that is, as a series of procedures falling along a continuum. One begins with the least intrusive or complex procedure deemed effective and gradually and carefully escalates or evolves to more intrusive procedures as it seems necessary.

Although clients rarely manifest a unitary, discrete behavioral deficit or excess, instead often showing a complicated pattern of both, for the purposes of clarity the evolution of interventions will be illustrated separately for these two ends of the behavioral continuum. The treatment of behavioral deficits will be discussed first, and the various procedures utilized are summarized in Table 4.1.

TREATMENT OF BEHAVIORAL DEFICITS—INTERVENTIONS

The treatment of behavioral deficits can take many forms: positive reinforcement, negative reinforcement, shaping, chaining, behavioral rehearsal, contracting, and token economy.

Table 4.1   SUMMARY OF CONTINGENCY MANAGEMENT: TREATMENT OF
BEHAVIORAL DEFICITS

	Intervention	Definition	Model reference
Less	Positive reinforcement	Administration of a positive reinforcer contingent on emission of target deficit	Bacon-Prue, Blount, Hosey, and Drabman (1980)
	Negative reinforcement	Removal of a negative reinforcer contingent on emission of target deficit	Blount, Baer, and Collins (1984)
Complexity or Intrusiveness	Shaping	Differential reinforcement of successive approximations	Hart, Reynolds, Baer, Brawley, and Harris (1968)
	Chaining	Component links added to a behavior chain in a backward order	Martin, Kehoe, Bird, Jensen, and Darbyshire (1971)
	Behavioral rehearsal	Modeling and role playing with corrective feedback	Edelstein and Eisler (1976)
	Contracting	Agreement specifying behaviors to be performed and reinforcers to be provided	Greene, Bailey, and Barber (1981)
More	Token economy	Conditioned reinforcers earned to be later cashed in	Jason (1984)

Martin and Pear (1978) state the first rule of remediating a deficiency: "If you want someone to do something, first try telling him" (p. 229). This is illustrated by an amusing anecdote retold by one of the authors. While working on his master's thesis at an institution for the retarded, he tried to utilize positive reinforcement to teach a woman who worked in the kitchen to stack plates and dishes in one area and cups and utensils in another. After several sessions with little or no progress, one of the nurses finally told the woman to "put the plates and dishes here and the cups and utensils over there" (p. 229). That was that!

Positive Reinforcement

However, it should be understood by this point that to *maintain* such a behavior change, the response must be followed by contingent positive reinforcement, the presentation of a contingent positive reinforcer.

To repeat Tennov's (1975) "3 R's Rule"—reinforced *r*esponses *r*ecur—if one wishes a behavioral response to be made more frequently, its emission must be followed by a reinforcing consequence: either *the administration of a positive reinforcer (positive reinforcement)* or *the withdrawal of a negative reinforcer (negative reinforcement)*. This is the essence of all operant-based treatment programs for the remediation of a behavioral deficit.

Walker and Shea (1980) state the five principles or rules of reinforcement that must be observed if the intervention is to be successful: (1) "Reinforcement must be dependent on the manifestation of the appropriate behavior"—that is, the reinforcer must be a contingent consequence. (2) "The appropriate behavior must be reinforced immediately" with as short a response-consequence interval as practical or feasible for more efficient learning. (3) "During initial stages of the behavior change process the appropriate behavior must be reinforced each time it is exhibited"—a continuous reinforcement schedule for more efficient learning. (4) "When the newly acquired behavior reaches a satisfactory frequency level, it should be reinforced intermittently" on a partial schedule of reinforcement for greater resistance to extinction and to postpone "reinforcer-satiation." (5) "Social reinforcers must always be applied with tangible reinforcers" to create effective and convenient conditioned reinforcers (pp. 22–24).

Before the implementation of any contingency management procedure involving positive reinforcement, *one must determine what that reinforcer will be,* as previously discussed in Chapter 2. Moreover, one should vary or change reinforcers frequently to maintain high reinforcer interest and strength and, therefore, the effectiveness of the contingency.

The reinforcer can be administered by the therapist, by others in the client's environment, or by the client. However, whoever administers it and whatever one chooses to administer, Martin and Pear (1978) reiterate the previously discussed warning, "A stimulus is defined as a reinforcer only by its effect on behavior" (p. 25).

For example, Bacon-Prue, Blount, Hosey, and Drabman (1980) publicly posted the photograph of each resident in a facility for the retarded who made his bed. The photo was attached to a poster entitled "The Bedmakers" and was on display for all to see for the remainder of the day. During the first 22 days that this contingency was in effect, the percentage of beds made rose from a mean of 21 percent during baseline to a mean of 64 percent. When the contingency was discontinued, the percentage of beds made declined to a mean of 49 percent, and when reinstated, rose to a mean of 71 percent. Residents were frequently observed to show off their posted pictures.

Stokes and Kennedy (1980) increased children's cooperation during dental treatment by rewarding only low levels of uncooperative behavior. Although their procedure was not novel, their reinforcer surely was. As the positive reinforcer, children received a small trinket, the capsule in which the silver-alloy amalgam was mixed—a natural waste product of the dental treatment and otherwise to be thrown away. In addition, as an example of the Premack principle, the cooperative child could raise the next child in the dental chair with the pneumatic foot pedal. Again in dentistry an equally effective and novel reinforcer was utilized with adults by Iwata and Becksfort (1981). To improve preventive dental care, a portion of the dental fee was refunded contingent on improvement in dental plaque scores. This reduction of fee could be viewed as an example of negative reinforcement—the reduction of an aversive stimulus.

Negative Reinforcement

Blount, Baer, and Collins (1984) worked with a severely myopic 11-year-old boy who was having difficulty complying with his required and lengthy daily visual training exercises. Using the apparent aversiveness inherent in the training situation (a negative reinforcer), the researchers told the boy "that sessions would no longer consist of 100 stimulus presentations, but instead would end when he reached criterion at an experimenter-determined distance. He was instructed that in order to shorten session length, he should attempt to score as well as possible" on the test (p. 54). Although length and number of trials were greatly reduced, there were simultaneous significant improvements in visual acuity. Compliance with the training exercises increased as a result of the contingency, with corresponding visual improvements.

Shaping

A major problem with contingent positive reinforcement arises when the target response to be reinforced is emitted either very infrequently or not at all. That is, there is virtually no response to reinforce because it is not in the client's behavioral repertoire. In these circumstances, the therapist could use such procedures as *instruction, modeling, guidance, prompts,* or the contingency management technique called **shaping**: the *differential reinforcement of successive approximations.* This procedure involves breaking down the ultimately desired response into many smaller sequential components, the simplest of which are exhibited by the client. Gradually, the therapist differentially reinforces closer and closer approximations of the final response.

Hart, Reynolds, Baer, Brawley, and Harris (1968) attempted to reinforce cooperative play in a 5-year-old preschool girl. However, because her rate of cooperative play was so low, "this behavior was shaped into her repertoire" (p. 73). At first, her teachers reinforced verbalizations near other children; eventually, verbalizations involving other children; and ultimately, actual cooperative play. Martin, Burkholder, Rosenthal, Tharp, and Thorne (1968), working with a population of adolescents homebound because of a variety of disruptive behaviors, gradually shaped appropriate school attendance. The preliminary behaviors that were reinforced included one to four hours of school attendance with no schoolwork required and at least one hour of good behavior. Intermediate behaviors included full-time attendance, some academic work, and no behavior that damaged property or injured people. Final treatment goal behaviors included schoolwork as assigned and no behavior that could not be tolerated in a classroom.

In a frequently referenced ("classic") study, Isaacs, Thomas, and Goldiamond (1960) shaped verbal behavior in a 40-year-old catatonic schizophrenic who had been mute for 19 years. Using chewing gum as the positive reinforcer, speech was reinstated over the course of six weeks by first requiring eye movement, then lip movement, then any vocalization, and finally closer successive approximations to actual language.

As another way to utilize a shaping procedure, Wulbert and Dries (1977) successfully worked with a hyperactive and greatly disruptive third-grade boy who exhibited aggression, noncompliance, and a variety of repetitive ritualistic behaviors involving his fingers and hands. As part of the reinforcement contingency, he was awarded poker chips (tokens) that could be exchanged for a variety of prizes. These tokens were contingent on "hands down" and "quiet behavior." At first, he received a token for each 15 seconds of appropriate behavior. "After 15 seconds of 'hands down,' [he] was handed a chip and told, 'Good, you have your hands down and you are quiet.' When [he] had succeeded in earning chips for three consecutive 15-second intervals, the time interval was lengthened to 30 seconds. According to the same criteria, the interval was lengthened to 45 seconds, 1 minute, and eventually to 3, 4, and 5 minute intervals" (p. 25). This shaping procedure allowed him to go for increasingly longer intervals without disruptive behaviors.

Chaining

Another procedure, similar to shaping and also designed to generate new responses, is **chaining**. Here, the final target behavior is divided into a sequence of responses called a chain. Each component link of the chain could be an already-existing behavior, but not in the particular fixed order or sequence. New responses are added to a behavior chain in a backward direction, starting with the last response—the one that is directly followed by reinforcement—and working toward the response ultimately made first and furthest from the reinforced end of the chain. Each response in the chain thus reinforces the previous response (the one that led to it) and acts as the stimulus for the next response (the one that follows it). Martin and Pear (1978) illustrate a behavior chain with the example of teaching a child to get dressed. The first response learned (which is the final reinforced response) is doing up the zipper; the last response learned (which is the first response to be emitted and the one furthest from completion) is taking the pants from the dresser. Each of the many intermediate responses (e.g., holding the slacks upright, putting one leg in, putting the other leg in, pulling the slacks up, etc.) forms the behavior chain.

Behavioral Rehearsal

An additional procedure used to add behaviors to a client's repertoire is **behavioral rehearsal**. Frequently employed in assertiveness training

(Edelstein & Eisler, 1976), behavioral rehearsal involves the client, therapist, and possibly others in role-playing various vignettes of situations found to be troublesome by the client. As compared to modeling, in which the client may passively observe the model, behavioral rehearsal requires the client to practice the new response—that is, imitate the model—in front of the therapist. "On the basis of such role-played behaviors . . . the therapist may opt to provide immediate corrective feedback . . . which would be followed by a second attempt on the part of the client. This procedure might be continued until both client and therapist agree that the response is appropriately assertive and is accompanied by minimal anxiety" (Rimm & Masters, 1979, p. 74).

Contracting

One of the common misconceptions regarding behavior modification in general is that because of its historical roots in basic learning theory, its practitioners treat their clients no differently than one would treat a rat, pigeon, or monkey, that is, in essentially a nonverbal fashion. Although a verbal explanation of the contingencies involved is not essential for their effectiveness (as shown by success with nonhuman subjects), a clear and explicit statement of the response required and the reinforcer to follow does enhance learning. Seidner and Kirschenbaum (1980) found that giving subjects information about treatment strategy and expected outcome in a contingency management situation produced both greater involvement and more behavior change than that found in control groups not receiving such information. The development of a **contract**, or *contingency contracting,* epitomizes the explicitness of the stated contingency.

Martin and Pear (1978) define a contract as "a very clear statement of what behaviors of what individuals will produce what reinforcers and who will deliver those reinforcers" (p. 376). To further clarify that statement, Walker and Shea (1980), among others, describe the principle involved as "Grandma's Law" and provide the following examples: "Eat your spinach and then you can have some ice cream," "Cut the lawn and then you can use the car," and "Write 27 articles and 10 books and then you will be promoted to professor" (p. 60).

The "if-then" relationship stated in a contract is for the "protection" of all parties involved. The negotiated and mutually agreed-on contract clearly defines the response to be emitted in terms of its operational definition and measures of frequency, duration, and/or intensity. There should be no confusion about what the required response is, when and how it should be made, and how to tell whether or not it was in fact made. The contingent reinforcement also must be explicitly spelled out. There should be no confusion about what the reinforcer is, when and how and by whom it is to be administered, and how to tell whether or not it was in fact administered. The contract can be succinctly stated or quite elaborate; it can be verbal or in writing. Many therapists prefer written contracts with children because of their more explicit nature and their ability to be prominently posted to act as a reminder to all parties involved. Walker and Shea (1980) give an example of a contract worksheet containing 24 sequenced tasks (steps) to perform in the development of a written contract and an example of a typical blank contract form to be used in an elementary school. See the Appendix for both of these forms and for actual client contracts.

The widespread use of contracts is quite evident in numerous "everyday" situations, for example, in agreements with employers, employees, and clients regarding services rendered and remuneration. Their popularity in clinical settings is equally high. Greene, Bailey, and Barber (1981) developed a contingency contract with children riding the school bus. The agreement reached was that if the duration and frequency of noise outbursts were reduced below the level of the previous day, then "high-appeal" taped music would be played and a prize raffle would be conducted. Hall, Baker, and Hutchinson (1977) found contracting useful as a therapeutic tool with former heroin addicts on methadone maintenance. They provided such reinforcers as home delivery of methadone, free tickets to special events, free bus tokens and lunches, and time off probation contingent on such behaviors as increased percentages of opiate-free urines and days on time to work. Using a similar population, McCaul, Stitzer, Bigelow, and Liebson (1984) also increased the percentage of opiate-free urine samples in their population with the following contracted agreement: Each opiate-free specimen on Monday and Friday would result in the awarding of $10, one take-home methadone dose, and the reduction of such clinic requirements as filling out questionnaires. An opiate-positive specimen would lead to the forfeiture of these reinforcements. "The experimental group consistently provided a higher percentage of opiate-free urines than did the control group throughout the intervention. Overall . . . almost 80% of the specimens from experimental patients were opiate free compared with 60% from the control patients" (pp. 38–39).

O'Leary, Pelham, Rosenbaum, and Price (1976) developed a contract agreement among a group of hyperkinetic children, their teachers, and their parents. Treatment for these hyperactive and disruptive children consisted of a carefully developed, home-based reward program with five components: (1) specification of daily classroom goals, (2) praise, (3) daily evaluation by the teacher, (4) daily report card sent to the parents, and (5) home reward. Daily goals were both academic and prosocial behaviors that needed to be increased. The researchers carefully worked with the parents to develop appropriate and motivating daily and weekly reinforcements. These were contingent on the teacher's report that the daily goals were met. Figure 4.1 illustrates just how well this contract worked. The effectiveness of the intervention can be seen in the dramatic reduction in the scores on the Problem Behavior Rating Scale, one of the dependent measures, between the pre- and posttests.

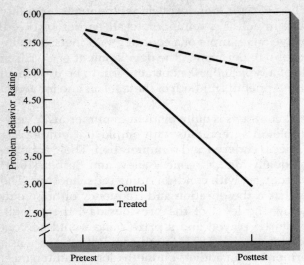

Figure 4.1 Comparison of the mean problem behavior ratings of nine hyperkinetic children treated with behavior therapy, and of eight similar controls. (*Source:* K. D. O'Leary, W. E. Pelham, A. Rosenbaum, & G. H. Price, Behavioral treatment of hyperkinetic children: an experimental evaluation of its usefulness, *Clinical Pediatrics, 15* (1976), 510–515. Copyright 1976 by J. B. Lippincott Co., Philadelphia. Reprinted by permission of the publisher.)

Token Economy

A still more complex or elaborate form of contingency contracting is the **token economy** (see Kazdin, 1977). Although it is clearly more complicated to design and implement a token economy, it helps control for several of the important drawbacks found with some of the other procedures. Most important, the delivery of primary positive reinforcement on either a continuous or partial schedule frequently presents some practical problems. A continuous reinforcement schedule (CRF) is often cumbersome and expensive to administer and can also lead to faster reinforcer satiation (one gets "tired of it"). This can result in lower reinforcer value and subsequent lower motivation. In addition, a CRF schedule produces less resistance to extinction (i.e., faster extinction) once reinforcement is withheld. Partial reinforcement schedules, on the other hand, often impose long delays between the response and the eventual primary reinforcement and, subsequently, may lead to extinction during acquisition.

The token economy bridges the gap between these two schedules by providing conditioned reinforcers on a continuous schedule and more primary reinforcers on a partial schedule. Under this system, tokens (originally neutral, often valueless stimuli such as checkmarks, stars, stickers, stamps, smiling faces, points, chips, play money, etc.) are administered, "banked," and ultimately "cashed in" for a variety of backup primary reinforcers. More valuable reinforcers frequently cost more tokens. Because they are used to buy reinforcers, the tokens themselves become conditioned reinforcers, capable of maintaining behavior. The utilization of money in most of the world's cultures is an "everyday" illustration of a token economy.

Brown, Fugua, and Otts (1986) stress the importance of pairing tokens with liberal amounts of verbal praise. Working with problem readers in an after-school tutoring program, they developed a token economy to encourage reluctant readers to "stick with" the required assignments. Along with the tokens (various decorative stickers), the tutors were instructed to verbalize such statements as "Joe, you paid attention and didn't miss a word. Good work! Here's a sticker" (p. 601). The combination appears to increase the reinforcing value of both the tokens and the verbal praise.

The clinical applications of the token economy range from the extremely elaborate (e.g., Ayllon & Azrin, 1968), where nearly every aspect of life on a mental hospital ward was involved, to somewhat less ambitious utilization. Ayllon and Azrin had patients earn points for a variety of carefully specified on- and off-ward jobs and self-care behaviors. Accumulated points were spent on an elaborate menu of reinforcers, including possessionals, response opportunities, and degrees of privacy. Moss and Rick (1981a) also utilized an extensive token economy system in a psychiatric hospital, this time with adolescents. The specific target behaviors were chosen because of their therapeutic value. They included attendance at group exercise classes and at both group and occupational therapy sessions. On a much smaller scale, Dapcich-Miura and Hovell (1979) improved adherence to a complex medical regimen by an elderly heart patient with the use of contingent tokens. This 82-year-old man, who had suffered a massive myocardial infarction and periodically experienced angina, earned tokens for taking walks to obtain physical exercise, drinking orange juice to increase potassium in his diet, and taking his required medications. Earned tokens were spent on selecting the dinner menu for the evening meal and the restaurant for a weekend dinner. As can be seen in Figure 4.2, the results of this intervention showed an increased adherence to all three aspects of his medical regimen when the token phase was in effect. As a positive side effect, a reduction in both family arguments and reported angina pain was also noted.

Jason (1984) used a token economy to reduce the amount of time seven children in one family spent watching television. The children earned tokens by engaging in a variety of more acceptable activities (school, play, and housework). They exchanged their tokens for predetermined amounts of TV viewing as well as to purchase a variety of additional backup reinforcers. The results showed that the TV viewing dropped from an average of 7.5 hours a day during baselevel to an average of only 3.7 hours a day during the intervention. Furthermore, "the mother indicated that with onset of the behavior program, her children began helping her

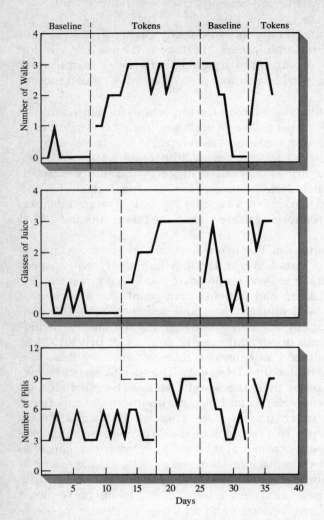

Figure 4.2 Number of adherence behaviors (walking, orange juice drinking, and pill taking) per day under repeated baseline and token reinforcement conditions. (*Source:* E. Dapcich-Miura & M. F. Hovell, Contingency management of adherence to a complex medical regimen in an elderly heart patient, *Behavior Therapy,* *10* (1979), 193–201. Copyright 1979 by the Association for Advancement of Behavior Therapy. Reprinted by permission of the publisher and the authors.)

with chores around the house. . . . The program helped the children switch from having leisure time activities which were television dominated to activities which were more interpersonal. The parents reported that the children played games with one another, developed new interests and began using their time in more creative ways" (p. 3).

As a novel and creative example of the utilization of tokens, Dachman,

Halasz, and Bickett (1984) successfully reduced the incidence of severe tantrum behavior by a 7-year-old child. They rewarded each 15 minutes without a tantrum by giving the child the opportunity to connect a dot (the "token") in a dot-to-dot picture puzzle. In addition, after a certain number of dots were connected, the child was reinforced with more tangible rewards administered through a "grab bag." This paper lunch bag contained slips of paper representing various activity, monetary, and edible reinforcers. It appears, therefore, that the total "reinforcement package" in this study consisted of a combination of primary reinforcers, conditioned reinforcers, possessionals and edibles, uncertainty reduction (each connected dot brings the child closer to solving the puzzle), and the Premack principle.

Token Economies and Economics

It is interesting to note the similarities between a token economy and a more traditional economic system. Kagel and Winkler (1972) state, "A token system for ward populations, whatever else it might happen to be, closely approximates the economist's concept of a closed economic system where tokens are money, deliveries of tokens as conditioned reinforcers are wage payments, and exchange rates of tokens for primary reinforcers are prices of consumption goods" (p. 335). As such, a new field—"behavioral economics"—should incorporate the effects of a variety of economic variables in the understanding of human behavior.

To explore this relationship further, Winkler (1973) developed a token economy (closed economic system) on a female chronic ward of a psychiatric hospital. The patients were predominantly diagnosed as having "schizophrenia" or "mental deficiency," and their average length of hospitalization was 12 years. Patients earned tokens for a variety of appropriate ward behaviors, including involvement in occupational and industrial therapy, daily exercises, and such self-care activities as showering and making their beds. Tokens were spent on a variety of items sold at the ward shop, such as candy and tea; for TV privileges; and for leaving the ward.

While the intervention was in effect, and the patients were earning, saving, and spending tokens, the token system had "a certain economic balance" (Winkler, 1973, p. 23). Winkler explained "balance" as "the discrepancy between total patient income and total patient expenditure. Total patient income is the total number of tokens given to patients in a specified time. Total patient expenditure is the total number of tokens patients spend during a specified period" (p. 23). "Savings" was represented by the number of tokens held by a given patient at a given time.

In a series of experimental manipulations, Winkler (1973) found that changes in the economic balance had marked and dramatic effects on the behaviors that earned tokens. As token expenditure exceeded income and, therefore, savings were reduced, there was an immediate improvement in reinforced token-earning behaviors. As token income exceeded expenditure and savings increased, there was a noted reduction in reinforced behaviors. This behavioral sensitivity to economic theory, therefore, needs to be taken into careful consideration when one develops and implements a token economy.

As with the treatment of behavioral deficits, there is a similar evolution or hierarchy of interventions for the treatment of behavioral excesses. These procedures are summarized in Table 4.2 and discussed below.

TREATMENT OF BEHAVIORAL EXCESSES—INTERVENTIONS

The treatment of behavioral excesses can involve such interventions as DRO, extinction, time-out, negative punishment, overcorrection, and positive punishment.

DRO

As with the treatment of behavioral deficits, there is a series of contingency management procedures, arranged in a hierarchy of complexity or intrusiveness, for the treatment of behavioral excesses. Derived from the

Table 4.2 SUMMARY OF CONTINGENCY MANAGEMENT: TREATMENT OF BEHAVIORAL EXCESSES

	Intervention	Definition	Model Reference
Less	Differential reinforcement of other behavior (DRO)	Administration of a positive reinforcer contingent on omission of target excess	Bennett (1980)
	Extinction	Elimination of the response-positive reinforcer contingency	Williams (1959)
Complexity or Intrusiveness	Time-out	Removal from reinforcing to nonreinforcing setting for specified time	Mace, Page, Ivancic, and O'Brien (1986)
	Negative punishment	Removal of a positive reinforcer contingent on emission of target excess	Forman (1980)
	Overcorrection	Performance of a behavior to overcorrect a misbehavior	Foxx and Azrin (1972)
More	Positive punishment	Administration of a negative reinforcer contingent on emission of target excess	Foxx, McMorrow, Bittle, and Bechtel (1986)

fact that behavioral deficits and excesses are on different ends of the same behavior continuum (an excess of out-of-seat behavior is a deficit of in-seat behavior), the first technique involves the utilization of all of the previously discussed procedures to increase the opposite and incompatible deficit. Known as **DRO**, the initials can stand for *d*ifferential *r*einforcement of *o*ther behavior, of *o*pposite behavior, or of *o*mission (see Tryon, 1976, and Woods, 1974). Rather than focusing on the *emission* of the target excess, one concentrates here on the *omission* of that response and/or on the *emission of some other response.* Redmon (1987) defines DRO, sometimes also referred to as "omission training," as a "procedure whereby a reinforcer is presented at the end of a predetermined time period only if a target behavior does not occur during that period" (p. 107).

Illustrations of this procedure, even in newspaper accounts, are easy to find. A local newspaper's classified ads department and a fuel oil company, both plagued by people who delay in paying their bills (target behavioral excess) gave cash discounts (reinforcement) to people who paid within ten days of billing (desired behavioral deficit). A high school, troubled with excessive absenteeism among both students and teachers, gave coupons worth hamburgers, T-shirts, gasoline, records, and dinners to those who attended on time. Police handed out "award" tickets to pedestrians who did not jaywalk. The focus in each of these cases is on strengthening some incompatible deficit, which, in turn, weakens the maladaptive excess.

Examples from the literature include the following: Vingoe (1980) reduced an excessive toilet ritual in a chronic obsessive-compulsive patient by increasing incompatible social behaviors (deficit) with weekend visits from his family as the reinforcement. In a previously described study, Dachman, Halasz, and Bickett (1984) reduced the incidence of tantrum behavior by rewarding each 15 minutes without a tantrum with the dot-to-dot picture. Redmon (1987) successfully reduced the frequency of aggressive and violent attacks by an 18-year-old developmentally disabled male living in a community group home by making various reinforcements contingent on five days without an attack. And Bennett (1980), combining DRO with shaping, reduced a retarded boy's habitual vomiting following meals. Additional food, praising, hugging, and scratching (the positive reinforcers) were contingent on gradually increasing intervals of not vomiting. Bennett stated that not only did this procedure work but also it "had none of the potential side effects of aversive techniques" (p. 17).

Acceptability of DRO   After reviewing the literature concerning DRO as well as the ethical and legal concerns raised by other techniques designed to reduce behavioral excesses, Homer and Peterson (1980) reiterated Bennett's feelings toward DRO. They concluded that "DRO schedules compare favorably with other techniques in speed and completeness of response elimination" (p. 449) and should be the preferred response elimination procedure. Similarly, Witt and Robbins (1985) surveyed teachers' attitudes about the acceptability of various classroom intervention strategies aimed at reducing inappropriate behaviors. The procedure rated highest in acceptability was DRO—rewarding acceptable alternative behaviors. Thus teachers ought to be willing to implement this procedure first as part of a classroom behavior management program. (Not surprisingly, Witt and Robbins found that corporal punishment was rated the least acceptable procedure by the surveyed teachers.) Similarly, Calvert and McMahon (1987) had 90 mothers of young children evaluate "the treatment acceptability of a behavioral parent training program" (p. 165). Although the overall program ratings were quite positive, all the reinforcement procedures aimed at increasing behavioral deficits were rated as more acceptable than any of the aversive procedures aimed at reducing behavioral excesses.

Bates and Wehman (1977) reviewed the literature on the behavioral treatment of six targeted maladaptive behaviors by the mentally retarded: aggressive behavior, self-injurious behavior, stereotypical behavior, classroom disruptive behavior, noncompliant behavior, and inappropriate social behavior. Of 11 different behavioral interventions examined, DRO was the most frequently used, found in more than 23 percent of the studies reviewed.

Although DRO has been found to be quite effective in the treatment of behavioral excesses, there are times when DRO alone either doesn't work or doesn't work fast enough in reducing the rate or frequency of a serious behavioral excess. In these cases, the following aversive procedures, arranged in increasing order along the intrusiveness hierarchy, are tried: extinction, time-out, negative punishment, overcorrection, and positive punishment. To be maximally effective, DRO should be used *concurrently* with these procedures to provide an appropriate behavior to take the place of the behavioral excess that is being eliminated. In fact, in reviewing a behavioral program written for a severely disturbed child, I noted that reinforcement for appropriate behavior (DRO) had to occur on a ratio of 10:1 to the administration of any of the more aversive procedures.

Extinction

Extinction involves the *withholding of reinforcement* following the emission of the target response. If a response is an operant, and if the reinforcer maintaining that response can be both determined and controlled, then the termination of that reinforcer should lead to the reduction or elimination of that response. This procedure involves the breaking of the response-consequence connection.

A classic illustration of extinction is found in Williams (1959), who eliminated "tyrant-like tantrum behavior" by a young boy who demanded special attention at bedtime. At baselevel, his parents spent up to two hours a night in his bedroom waiting for him to fall asleep; they were instructed simply not to reenter his room contingent on his screaming once he was put to bed for the night. Figure 4.3 shows a graphic representation of the extinction process from the Williams study. The length of time the child cried is graphed for each of the times the parents put him to bed and did not reenter. It will be noted that crying was reduced to only a few minutes within three to four nights and to no crying within seven nights. An interesting phenomenon, however, then occurred. "About a week later, [he] screamed and fussed after an aunt put him to bed, probably reflecting spontaneous recovery of the tantrum behavior. The aunt then reinforced the tantrum behavior by returning to [his] bedroom and remaining there until he went to sleep" (p. 269). The author then extinguished this behavior a second time. As the graph illustrates, this second extinction, too, only required seven sessions. The possibility and course of spontaneous recovery are important to note. If unexpected, it may appear as if something drastically wrong with the intervention is happening and that perhaps it should be abandoned. This is not the case.

Another important phenomenon anyone who implements an extinction procedure should note is that the course of extinction is not always as quick or smooth as that found by Williams. Wright, Brown, and Andrews (1978) extinguished ruminative vomiting (regurgitation of food with inter-

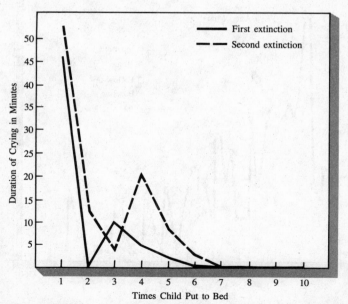

Figure 4.3 Length of crying in two extinction series as a function of successive occasions of being put to bed. (*Source:* C. D. Williams, The elimination of tantrum behavior by extinction procedures, *Journal of Abnormal and Social Psychology,* 59 (1959), 269. Copyright 1959 by the American Psychological Association. Reprinted by permission of the publisher and the author.)

mittent rechewing, swallowing, and expectoration) by a hospitalized young girl diagnosed as failing to thrive and malnourished. After noting that staff members frequently rushed to her and picked her up after an episode of rumination, it was decided to try to extinguish this life-threatening response by eliminating the possible reinforcer. After nine days of baselevel, hospital personnel were instructed to put the girl down and leave the area for three minutes following each episode of rumination. As Figure 4.4 shows, although there was an eventual reduction in rumination, the rate at first rose and the behavior became more variable and intense. Only gradually did the response rate decrease.

This extinction-induced initial rise in rate and intensity of behavior (the so-called "extinction burst") creates at least two problems, especially if they are not anticipated. First, the person implementing the extinction may think the technique is not working and thus abandon the procedure long before success would have been obtained. Second, the quantitative and qualitative increases in the behavior (e.g., tantrum, regurgitation) are frequently difficult to tolerate. Occasionally, therefore, the interventionist (e.g., parent, teacher) can't help "giving in." This capitulation produces intermittent reinforcement, increasing resistance to extinction and thus making subsequent extinction even more difficult.

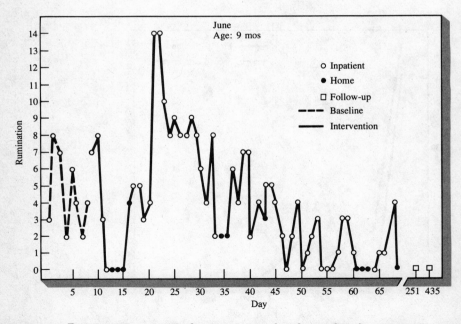

Figure 4.4 Ruminative vomiting frequency per day during baseline, intervention (extinction), and follow-up. (*Source:* D. F. Wright, R. A. Brown, & M. E. Andrews, Remission of ruminative vomiting through a reversal of social contingencies, *Behaviour Research and Therapy, 16* (1978), 134–136. Copyright 1978 by Pergamon Press, Ltd. Reprinted by permission of the publisher and the authors.)

Sensory Extinction   Since the theoretical basis of extinction is the removal of response-contingent reinforcement, one needs to consider carefully and evaluate all the various possible reinforcers that might serve to maintain the behavior. The previously described sensory-reinforcement model developed by Kish (1966) talks of the "reinforcing effects of the sensory consequences of the behavior" itself (p. 110). If this is the case—that is, if visual and auditory consequences of behavior act to maintain that behavior—removal of these sensory reinforcers is necessary as a part of the extinction procedure. Toward this end, Aiken and Salzberg (1984) implemented what they called **sensory extinction**. They hypothesized that some of the stereotypic responses found in, for example, autistic individuals may, in fact, be operant behavior maintained by its sensory consequences. In other words, the auditory stimulation resulting from aberrant vocalizations, clapping hands, and dropping objects may work to maintain these behaviors. If so, removal of the auditory, visual, and/or proprioceptive consequences of autistic behaviors might lead to their extinction.

To test this theory, Aiken and Salzberg (1984) chose a 9-year-old autistic boy with an auditory stereotypic behavior referred to as a "slur"—"a sloshing or slurring sound made with the lips, teeth, and tongue" (p. 293). To remove the possibly reinforcing sensory consequences of this behavior, they fitted the child with earphones through which "white noise" could be played to mask the slur. Figure 4.5 shows that the percentage of timed intervals in which a slur was noted decreased from approximately 60 percent during baselevel to less than 20 percent during the white noise, sensory-extinction phase. The authors concluded, "Perhaps the stereotypic vocalizations were, indeed, maintained by their auditory sensory consequences, and, thus, masking them with white noise led to their extinction" (pp. 297–298).

Time-Out

The extinction procedure, however useful, may not work when the target response is not an operant (i.e., is not maintained by its consequences), when the reinforcer for the response cannot be either determined or eliminated, or when the response has to be modified quickly because of its severity. In these circumstances, the next more intrusive procedure, still to be used concurrently with DRO, is **time-out**.

Time-out is defined as "the removal (of a person) from an apparently reinforcing setting to a presumably non-reinforcing setting for a specified and limited period of time" (Walker & Shea, 1980, p. 79). It has been used to treat, among many other behaviors, frequent complaints of stomach-ache by a 10-year-old girl (Miller & Kratochwill, 1979), conduct problems (noncompliance, tantrums, talking back, fighting) in children ages 2 to 7 (Roberts, Hatzenbuehler, & Bean, 1981), delusional and hallucinatory speech (Davis, Wallace, Liberman, & Finch, 1976), and self-injurious behavior (Tate & Baroff, 1966).

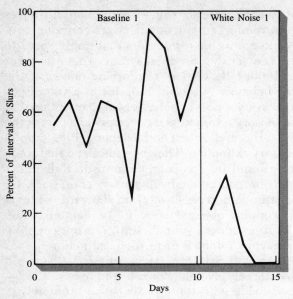

Figure 4.5 The percentage of three-second intervals in which "slurs" occurred across all experimental conditions for subject 1. (*Source:* J. M. Aiken & C. L. Salzberg, The effects of a sensory extinction procedure on stereotypic sounds of two autistic children, *Journal of Autism and Developmental Disorders, 14,* (1984), 291–299. Copyright 1984 by Plenum Publishing Corporation. Reprinted by permission of the publisher and the authors.)

Kazdin (1980), speaking of the several variations of time-out, says that "perhaps the most commonly used (and abused) version is isolation of a client in a time-out room. Isolation is an exclusionary form of time-out because the client is excluded from the situation and setting in which the disruptive behavior occurred" (p. 331). With another variation, the client is allowed to remain in the setting but is not permitted to receive reinforcers. This distinction between seclusion and time-out from positive reinforcement is an important one. "Time-out may be accomplished by ignoring an individual or expressly eliminating a major source of ongoing reinforcement. . . . Seclusion implies that the individual is insulated from many sources of ongoing stimulation including even the observation of reinforcing events or contact with other individuals" (Rimm & Masters, 1979, pp. 346–347).

Various Types of Time-Out   Rolider and Van Houten (1985), after reviewing the literature, describe time-out as a set of broadly defined techniques that can be applied in a variety of ways and settings. The common feature, however, is a reduction in the amount of reinforcement received during the time-out interval. In fact, the efficacy of time-out is proportional to the net reduction in reinforcement between the "time-in" and time-out periods. Toward this end, they note the importance of removing all sources of reinforcement during the time-out period, including self-stimulation. They describe a "movement suppression" time-out procedure as a means of reducing this type of potential reinforcement as well.

Griffiths, Bigelow, and Liebson (1977) similarly compared the efficacy of "activity time-out" and "social time-out" procedures in suppressing ethanol self-administration in alcoholics. Male alcoholics in a residential research ward had free access to alcohol except for the constraint that at least a 40-minute delay must elapse between drinks. Following the establishment of an alcohol consumption baselevel, the investigators manipulated the type of time-out during the 40-minute delay interval. During social time-out, each drink resulted in a 40-minute time-out from social interactions. Patients were not allowed to talk, gesture, or interact with other patients. Activity time-out involved 40 minutes of sitting in a chair and refraining from all overt activities except for socializing. Social time-out (the least effective manipulation) produced a mean suppression of alcohol consumption to 71 percent of baselevel; activity time-out produced a mean suppression to 36 percent of baselevel; and both activity and social time-out combined (the most effective manipulation) produced a mean suppression to 24 percent of baselevel.

The effective duration of a time-out period has been investigated by several researchers. No consistent findings, however, have been obtained. Although Barton, Guess, Garcia, and Baer (1970) and Sachs (1973) successfully modified maladaptive behaviors with time-out periods as short as 15 seconds and 30 seconds, respectively, Burchard and Barrera (1972) found that a 30-minute time-out period was more effective than a 5-minute period. Moreover, although White, Nielson, and Johnson (1972) found that both 15-minute and 30-minute time-out periods were more effective than a 1-minute period, the two longer periods were not significantly different from one another.

Mace, Page, Ivancic, and O'Brien (1986) describe time-out with contingent delay: "an extension of the time-out interval for a specified period of time contingent on the occurrence of aberrant behavior during time-out" (p. 79). Most commonly, a 2-minute time-out period would be extended for an additional 15 seconds each time a specified undesirable behavior was emitted during the final 15 seconds of the time-out period. Using mentally retarded children with severe behavior disorders, Mace and colleagues compared the efficacy of time-out both with and without contingent delay. The results showed that both measures reduced the targeted behaviors to comparable levels. There were no consistent differences; the contingent delay procedure "was not found to enhance time-out efficacy" (p. 83). The authors note the importance of their study since contingent delay is so frequently employed. When this procedure is used, they argue, some individuals may be needlessly retained in time-out for lengthy periods of time. This practice raises obvious ethical concerns.

Regardless of the specific parameters employed, Rimm and Masters (1979) also warn that "as with other techniques of aversive control, time-out procedures raise a certain degree of ethical concern. Time-outs of too long a duration and time-outs that have no built-in rules to allow interruption for legitimate reasons . . . are certainly inappropriate and examples of misuse. . . . There are safety factors that must be taken into account" (p. 346).

Hobbs, Walle, and Caldwell (1984) implemented brief parent (mother) training programs aimed at reducing noncompliant conduct problems in young children. One group was taught a social reinforcement procedure (essentially DRO) in which praise was contingent on the child's compliance. The other group was taught a time-out procedure, contingent on the child's noncompliance, in which a child was placed in the corner of the treatment room and attention and toys were removed for two minutes. Following training and the implementation of the programs, the mothers were asked to complete a Treatment Evaluation Inventory, giving their opinions of the treatments. "Results indicate that in addition to producing greater reductions in non-compliant behavior, time-out is rated as comparable in acceptability as social reinforcement. . . . This finding presents a generally positive view of parents' likelihood of participating in clinic treatment programs that incorporate time-out procedures as well as willingness to implement such procedures in the home setting" (pp. 135–136).

Negative Punishment

Again, as with the other techniques, results (or lack of results) sometimes require still further escalation of procedures. When all else has been tried and failed, DRO is used concurrently with more aversive procedures. Negative punishment, less severe than positive punishment, should be utilized first. Also known as *response cost*, this procedure involves the *removal of a positive reinforcer contingent on the emission of the behavioral excess*. With an 8-year-old profoundly retarded female who was quite disruptive on her bus ride to school, "music was played during each bus ride as long as the subject was sitting appropriately, and interrupted contingent upon each response defined as disruptive bus riding" (Barmann, Croyle-Barmann, & McLain, 1980, p. 693). This procedure resulted in a significant decrease in such behaviors. Similarly, Forman (1980) reduced the incidence of various disruptive and aggressive behaviors (e.g., hitting, kicking, shoving, throwing objects at someone, destroying someone else's property, and cursing) by a population of elementary school children by "fining" them each time these behaviors occurred. The children met with two graduate students twice a week for 30 minutes to play ball or listen to records and dance. Each incident of aggression resulted in a 2-minute reduction in this special time.

Hogan and Johnson (1985) present the major negative aspects of a response-cost program. These arise from the fact that it is clearly a punishment (i.e., aversive) procedure. Hogan and Johnson conclude, "It undoubt-edly stimulates the development of negative attitudes toward those ad-ministering it. Anyone who has ever had to pay a traffic fine or parking ticket could testify to this. . . . Clients [may] find many innovative ways to express their opposition to the rehabilitative goals of staff members [and] we should expect that the more negative their attitudes toward staff mem-bers, the more they would be motivated to rebel against their demands. Also, excessive use of response cost as a negative contingency may result in a reduction of the reinforcing value of the positive contingencies used. Why should one work if one's earnings are probably going to be consumed by fines?" (p. 88). In their research, Hogan and Johnson followed a baseline period by the implementation of concurrent token economy and re-sponse-cost programs. In the token economy, various appropriate behav-iors earned points, which were later spent for reinforcing goods or activi-ties. With response cost, infractions of the rules resulted in point fines. The results clearly show that these two interventions led to behavioral im-provement. However, eventual elimination of the response-cost compo-nent (while maintaining the token economy) led to still further improve-ments. Moreover, the general tone of the staff-client encounters became noticeably more positive and friendly during the phase when staff mem-bers were only paying tokens instead of also taking them away.

Overcorrection

The next more aversive procedure in the hierarchy is **overcorrection**. Schaefer and Millman (1981) describe this contingent aversive procedure as "having to perform another behavior which serves to correct or 'over-correct' the misbehavior. The corrective behavior should be related in some way to the misbehavior, follow immediately and be actively per-formed for a relatively long period of time" (p. 118). Lutzker and Martin (1981) state that "overcorrection involves restitution (correcting the con-sequences of maladaptive behavior, including at times to excess) and posi-tive practice (requiring that a related appropriate behavior be practiced, at times to excess)" (p. 221).

For example, Foxx and Azrin (1972) treated a mentally retarded fe-male resident of an institution whose aggressive and disruptive behaviors included throwing and overturning furniture. The overcorrection method required that she apologize to and reassure the other residents, make or smooth out all the beds, straighten up and clean all furniture on the ward, and sweep and mop the floors. Graphic representation of the data illus-trates a dramatic reduction of the target maladaptive behavioral excess.

Positive Punishment

When the response to be eliminated is disruptive or injurious and nothing else seems to work, DRO plus positive punishment procedures are used.

These are procedures of last resort, to be thought through, discussed, and reviewed before they are implemented. Although often effective, these aversive procedures raise various ethical and legal issues (to be discussed in more detail in Chapter 7). As with any therapeutic procedure, the client's right to refuse or discontinue treatment is an important issue. This issue is paramount in regard to aversives because they can often generate various emotional reactions, such as anxiety, fear, and anger, toward the environment and people involved in their administration. Moreover, and perhaps most important, positive punishment can be abused, resulting in possible physical harm to the client.

Some of the *aversive stimuli* that have been *presented to a client contingent on the emission of the target excess* include a three-second sound blast through a speaker into the ear for increased frequency of nocturnal bruxism (Heller & Strang, 1973), white noise through stereo headphones during the projection of slides depicting undesirable behavior (Matesanz, 1982), a fine mist at room temperature sprayed on the face by a plastic plant sprayer for self-injurious behaviors (hand biting, skin tearing, head banging) (Dorsey, Iwata, Ong, & McSween, 1980), contingent exercise (standing up and sitting down a number of times) for inappropriate verbal and aggressive behaviors (Luce, Delquadri, & Hall, 1980), and aromatic ammonia held under the nose for three seconds for hyperventilation (Singh, Dawson, & Gregory, 1980).

Treatment of Last Resort   Foxx, McMorrow, Bittle, and Bechtel (1986), working at the Anna Mental Health and Development Center, present a carefully developed punishment procedure that takes many patient safeguards into consideration. They note that the use of such punishment procedures as contingent electric shock ranks highest in terms of aversiveness, intrusiveness, and restrictiveness. However, when the maladaptive behavior is so serious that self-harm or injury to others is likely to occur, when the behavior is long-standing or durable, when it has withstood other attempts to treat it, when it prevents effective programming for appropriate behaviors, and when it results in the necessity of physical or chemical restraint or one-to-one staff attention, punishment may be the only alternative available. The authors describe a 20-year-old male patient who had been hospitalized in five different institutions since age 7 and previously diagnosed as "intermittent explosive disorder," "mild mental retardation," "bilateral deafness," "noncompliant," and "aggressive." Prior treatments included time-out, various medications, overcorrection, DRO, relaxation, restraint, exercise, isolation, and token economy. He continued to threaten, pinch, kick, hit, and pull hair. After a consent document was signed by the Human Rights and Behavior Management Committees of the institution, the parents, the facility's superintendent, and the state director of mental health, a punishment procedure involving electric shock to the back of his upper arms was implemented. (In addition to the shock, both time-out and DRO were used concurrently.) The program involved a 33-day period of high-intensity training during which episodes of the targeted behavior were punished by contingent shock.

The results showed that hair pulling, other aggression, and property destruction decreased to near zero and remained at that level during the one-year follow-up period. Moreover, a variety of appropriate social behaviors began to increase in frequency. The patient began to participate in such activities as outings, unescorted walks, holidays with his parents, and vocational training. At the time of the one-year follow-up, he had not suffered any physical injuries, was medication-free, and was being considered for a community-based vocational workshop. Apparently, the punishment procedure—viewed as a last resort—worked in this case.

I also reviewed a proposal to implement positive punishment to eliminate a life-long history of self-injurious behavior (SIB) in a severely retarded nonverbal woman. The SIB consisted of repeatedly slamming her forearm into her temple and then dragging it across her eye. She quickly broke the skin on her head and arm and became bloody. Baselevel recording indicated that she had hit herself as frequently as 423 times in a 16-minute period. Numerous treatments, including extinction, DRO, response cost, time-out, overcorrection, relaxation, and mild positive punishment, had all failed. At the time this proposal was written, she was medicated and kept in physical restraints for her own protection. Because of the severity and long history of the SIB, the proposed intervention involved contingent leg slapping—a quick slap to the thigh. In addition to various medical safeguards, a high-density, continuous reinforcement DRO procedure would simultaneously be implemented. Reinforcers would include edibles, hugs, rubs, shoulder massaging, head stroking, various objects, and the verbalization "Good." With all the precautions in place, the proposed intervention was approved.

The concurrent use of DRO with *all* these aversive procedures is necessitated by the fact that extinction, time-out, overcorrection, and punishment—although effective in reducing the frequency of the excessive behavior—do not teach or enhance the development of an appropriate substitute behavior. DRO is so effective and essential because it replaces the inappropriate, undesired behavior with a more appropriate and acceptable one for which the subject receives reinforcement.

TREATMENT OF BEHAVIORAL INAPPROPRIATENESS

The third category of maladaptive behaviors that can be treated with contingency management consists of **stimulus control problems**. These arise from making what might otherwise be an appropriate response in an inappropriate time or place. This *behavioral inappropriateness* is nicely illustrated by the nursery school teacher who said to one of the children shouting in the classroom, "You're speaking in an outside voice, but we're inside now."

Martin and Pear (1978) say that the "procedure by which we learn to emit appropriate behavior in the presence of the 'right' stimuli, and not in the presence of the 'wrong' stimuli, is called stimulus-discrimination training. Basically, this procedure involves reinforcing a response in the presence of one stimulus and not reinforcing the response (in other words, extinguishing it) in the presence of other stimuli" (pp. 104–105). If this is done a sufficient number of times, the behavior will be more likely to occur in the presence of the appropriate stimulus (called the "discriminative stimulus") and less likely to occur in the presence of the inappropriate stimulus. That is, one learns not only what responses to make through the use of contingent consequences but also when or where to make those responses. The basic operant principle of "reinforced responses recur" still holds true.

In the beginning stages of **stimulus-discrimination training**, it is often desirable to maximize or exaggerate the differences between the appropriate and inappropriate stimulus conditions in order to facilitate efficient learning. In a therapeutic setting, this process can be accomplished through a discussion that highlights the relevant characteristics of the different situations and the corresponding appropriate behavior. For example, I viewed a videotaped training session in which a group of retarded adults was being taught the difference between the appropriate and inappropriate places to engage in such behavior as tucking one's shirt into one's pants. Group members were shown photos of individuals engaged in such a behavior in either an appropriate or inappropriate setting. The discussion that followed the presentation of each pair of photos was aimed at delineating the relevant differences between the two locations.

I also had the opportunity to treat behavioral inappropriateness involving the "amorous" behaviors of a developmentally disabled adult female. Once the notion of "appropriateness" was established, the aim of therapy in part was to increase the number of times she asked herself the following questions: "Is this the appropriate time and place for this behavior?" and "Am I with the appropriate person for this behavior?"

In sum, a behavior need not be a problem only in terms of frequency, duration, and intensity for it to be considered maladaptive; setting must also be taken into consideration.

CASE STUDY

The following is an actual case study illustrating the model of concurrent behavior modification interventions described in this chapter.

When first observed, "George" was a 20-year-old male at a private special education high school. Testing showed that he was functioning at a sixth-grade academic level and had an IQ of 87. School records indicated that his behavior problems were first observed in kindergarten and that he had been in various schools and special classes since that time. He had

been previously diagnosed as "autistic," having a "personality disturbance," "childhood schizophrenic," and having "organic involvement."
Current behavioral observation indicated that George frequently bit his
left thumb (and it was scarred); plucked out his eyebrows and eyelashes
(trichotillomania) and, at this point, had virtually nothing left of either;
made "funny" faces and "animal noises"; and engaged in a minimum of
socialization with other students at school and no socialization outside of
school. He performed a minimum of independent behaviors at home and
was extremely dependent on his mother for all his basic and recreational
needs.

Assessment indicated that George most frequently plucked out his
hair at home, when bored, and that his parents responded with anger.
Although his parents made several "deals" with him regarding his plucking ("You can't go to California unless your eyebrows grow in!"), they
failed to live up to these ultimatums. He, similarly, made his noises and
faces predominantly in the presence of his mother. He stated that he
"teases her" in this way and that she frequently replied, "Oh, grow up!"
His finger biting seemed to be elicited by frustration or anger at not being
allowed to do something he wanted (e.g, going to the YMCA to swim), and
as the consequence of his biting, his mother usually gave in ("O.K., go
swimming").

Based on the assessment, it was decided that George manifested multiple behavioral deficits and excesses and that intervention should focus on
both. His deficits included his lack of socializing and other peer-oriented
and independent behaviors as well as his lack of an appropriate anger
and/or frustration response. His excesses included his biting and plucking
as well as his inappropriate noises and faces. A variety of contingency
management procedures were implemented to be used concurrently. His
excesses would be treated by DRO, extinction, and response cost. His
deficits would be treated by positive reinforcement, shaping, contracting,
token economy, and behavioral rehearsal.

After a discussion of the conditions affecting George's problems, his
parents were instructed in the principles of extinction. They were both to
ignore his plucking, noises and faces, and biting and, at the same time, try
not to acquiesce to his demands simply because of his biting. Simultaneously, a program of modeling and behavioral rehearsal was begun to
teach George more appropriate, verbal ways to express his displeasure and
desires. These new behaviors were to be reinforced by his parents.

A contract was then drawn up regarding his hair plucking. Every
other day he and his parents were to have a "hair check." Diagrams of his
eyebrow and eyelash areas were to be marked, showing existing hairs
(there were so few, they could easily be counted). A "positive" hair check
was one in which there were the same number of hairs or more as compared to the previous check. A "negative" hair check was one in which
there were fewer hairs than the last time. Positive hair checks were rewarded by stars on a calendar, which were cashed in for the privilege of

going swimming (determined to be a potent positive reinforcer). The number of stars required per swim was gradually increased (i.e., shaped) to three.

An additional contract was developed that paid him money (up to $10/week) for engaging in a variety of appropriate behaviors at home and school. He could earn a certain amount of money on a daily basis for such behaviors as eating lunch with another student, shooting pool in the school recreation hall, and working out in the school gym. At home, he earned money for a variety of chores (e.g., bringing in the mail and taking out the trash) that he now performed by a stated time of day without parental reminders. Before the intervention his parents periodically gave him non-contingent money. He now spent his earned money for such activities as bowling with the school and snacks after lunch. He was also taught how to go to the local shopping mall and, for example, buy lunch at a fast-food restaurant. This behavior was strongly socially reinforced.

By describing his "psychological problem" in terms of behavioral deficits and excesses, a specific series of contingency management procedures could thus be implemented. By week 15, George was consistently earning three positive hair-check stars a week and between $9.50 and $10.00 a week on his activity contract. The dramatic improvement in his behavior was noted by his parents as well as his school.

Chapter
5

Health Psychology and Biofeedback

In previous chapters of this text, the broad spectrum of application of behavior modification has been stressed. That is, the use of behavioral procedures with a wide variety of client populations and in numerous treatment settings has been illustrated with many examples from the professional literature. Their historical origins and solid grounding in basic operant conditioning have always been noted. This chapter discusses the expansion of these techniques into a relatively new field called **health psychology**. No more than about 10 or 15 years old (health psychology became a formal division of the American Psychological Association in 1978), health psychology (or "behavioral medicine" or "psychosomatic medicine") has been defined as ". . . the clinical use of techniques derived from the experimental analysis of behavior—behavior therapy and behavior modification—for the evaluation, prevention, management, or treatment of physical disease or physiological dysfunction" (Pomerleau & Brady, 1979, p. xii). Schwartz and Weiss (1977) describe the definition and goals of this field as the "development of behavioral-science knowledge and techniques relevant to the understanding of physical health and illness and the application of this knowledge to diagnosis, prevention, treatment and rehabilitation" (p. 379).

It should be stressed at this point that although health psychology appears to have the same goals as "traditional" medicine, its methods and "philosophies" are clearly different. Whereas the predominant treatment strategies employed by physicians are pharmacology and surgery, the health psychologist employs a whole host of "behavior change" procedures epitomized by behavior modification. Tulkin and Frank (1985), in their article entitled "The Changing Role of Psychologists in Health Maintenance Organizations" (HMOs), stress the "potential for psychologists ... to participate in the treatment of various medical conditions that entail behavior change as a critical part of the recovery process" (p. 1125). They list some of these specific medical problems as "chronic pain, eating disorders, hypertension ... heart disease, addiction ... and a variety of diseases for which compliance with medical regimens is a significant issue" (p. 1125).

It should also be noted here that health psychology is not to be viewed as in an either/or competition with traditional medicine. It is not the latest fad or "quackery" trying to replace tried-and-true medical treatment. It is, instead, the beginning of a new partnership. It is the realization that each discipline has its own expertise and that the different methodologies can work together in the overall care and treatment of the client. This collaboration is especially necessary in view of the estimates that between 50 percent and 65 percent of all "medical" complaints seen by general practitioners turn out to be "psychological" in nature (i.e., anxiety, tension, stress, or depression related) (Broskowski, 1981).

The scope of health psychology illustrated in this chapter will be divided into three parts: (1) the prevention of disease through risk-factor modification, (2) adherence to treatment regimens, and (3) the management of various specific medical disorders through behavioral techniques. Each is illustrative of the field of health psychology and will be dealt with separately.

RISK-FACTOR MODIFICATION

Obesity

Reporting on a National Institutes of Health conference, Burton and Foster (1985) conclude that "while most public attention and significant economic activity related to obesity had been devoted to cosmetic and aesthetic concerns about body weight, increasing evidence had accumulated in the scientific literature of the harmful medical (and psychological) consequences of being overweight and of its effects on longevity" (p. 1117). Obesity is now clearly associated with a variety of medical problems, including varicose veins, diabetes, surgical complications, hypertension, and coronary heart disease. The incidence of each of these disorders thus could be reduced by a reduction of the **risk factor**. Although there are a number of factors involved in the etiology of obesity—and each case should, therefore, be viewed individually—most behavioral treatment programs include a number of common elements.

Stunkard and Berthold (1985) list 49 of the most commonly used weight-control techniques, divided into seven major categories. Thirty-one of these procedures, stated as "tips" or suggestions, are "derived from the traditional applied behavioral analysis of the *antecedents* of a behavior, the *behavior* itself, and its *consequences*" (p. 823). That is, they involve modifying the stimulus conditions in which the eating occurs (e.g., eat only at regularly scheduled times and in the same place), the actual eating behavior (e.g., slow the rate of eating and leave some food on the plate), and the consequences of the eating (e.g., use reinforcement for meeting specific goals and enlist the social support of significant others). Support by parents is extremely important in treating childhood obesity.

Noting that "child and adolescent obesity is recognized as an important public health problem with the majority of overweight children becoming obese adults" (p. 91), Johnson and Corrigan (1987) developed a behavioral treatment program specifically for this population. Their program, in part, involves stimulus control of antecedent conditions; control of eating behaviors themselves; substitution of alternative, incompatible behaviors; and the development of a realistic physical exercise regimen. In all aspects of the program parental involvement is stressed, both as a role model and as the provider of reinforcement. Johnson and Corrigan note that "immediate praise, toys, and desired activities . . . contingent upon achievement of changes in eating and exercise habits are important elements in the program" (p. 95).

Working with a 7-year-old boy suffering from Prader-Willi syndrome—life-threatening obesity characterized by early development of hyperphagia, probably of hypothalamic origin—Jackson, Carlson, and Treiber (1987) developed a treatment plan that could be implemented by the boy's mother at home. The major components of this program included adherence to a strict diet, stimulus-control strategies, behavioral rehearsal of various appropriate eating behaviors, and the posting of a graph depicting weekly weighings. In order "to promote adherence to the diet plan, the family was instructed in the use of a token reinforcement system in which [the boy] earned stars for compliance during morning, after-school, and evening time periods. Stars were exchanged at the end of the week for an activity or tangible reinforcer" (p. 117).

Research has found that a regular exercise program, such as the use of a stationary bicycle, enhances the efficacy of almost all weight-loss programs. For example, Perri, McAdoo, McAllister, Lauer, and Yancey (1986) found that a group receiving traditional behavioral methods of weight control plus aerobic exercise lost significantly more weight than the standard behavioral group alone.

Finally, Hartwell, Kaplan, and Wallace (1986) examined the relationship between a weight-loss program and the control of diabetes mellitus. Using a population of non–insulin-dependent diabetics, the researchers compared diet, exercise, diet and exercise, and educational control groups in the management of their disorder. Among other procedures, the diet group "monitored their eating behavior through the use of a diary and learned stimulus control by identifying external cues which lead to overeating or to the consumption of inappropriate foods. They were instructed in self-administration of positive reinforcement and modification of environmental cues for eating" (p. 451). Results indicated that over a six-month period, the diet group showed the greatest reduction in both weight and blood glucose—which could, the researchers conclude, affect the diabetes beneficially. (Interestingly, in this study the diet-plus-exercise group did not do as well as the diet-alone group. The researchers believe this finding to be the result of compliance problems in this group, which simply did not adhere to the regimen. See the section on Adherence to Treatment Regimens.)

Smoking

Bernstein and Glasgow (1979), referring to a 1975 report by the World Health Organization (WHO), conclude that "smoking-related diseases are the major cause of disability and premature death in developed countries and that the control of smoking could do more to prolong life and improve health than any other single action in the whole field of preventive medicine" (p. 233). Cigarette smoking has been clearly linked to lung cancer, coronary heart disease, respiratory diseases, and decreased fetal development among many other medical problems. What is obviously needed is effective smoking-cessation programs.

Behavioral techniques for the control of smoking have focused on two major approaches: "(a) those designed to directly limit or suppress smoking and (b) those designed to increase and sustain non-smoking" (Walen, Hauserman, & Lavin, 1977, p. 119). The former include stimulus-control techniques to reduce the antecedents for smoking; response-cost techniques to mildly punish smoking; and more aversive procedures such as unpleasant covert imagery, electric shock, and aversion by satiation to smoky air, referred to as the "rapid smoking technique." The latter techniques, those designed to increase nonsmoking, include positive reinforcement of nonsmoking and of incompatible behaviors, public commitments to stop smoking, and such self-control procedures as the rehearsal of reasons to quit smoking. Incompatible behaviors like physical exercise or relaxation training are frequently reinforced as well. Positive reinforcement includes contingency contracting, token economy, monetary rewards, and any of the variety of procedures previously discussed in this text.

ADHERENCE TO TREATMENT REGIMENS

Both in psychological and medical practice, "clinicians know that getting patients to follow treatment recommendations is the bottom line. . . . Most procedures . . . would be only useless exercises if patients did not comply with prescribed therapeutic regimens. . . . Despite the obvious reliance on compliance as an important part of most therapeutic regimens, considerable evidence exists that patients often do not comply. . . . Problems with compliance occur across a range of medical and nonmedical regimens from appointment keeping to preventive regimens to treatment" (Levy, 1987, p. 567). For example, recall the previously mentioned study by Hartwell, Kaplan, and Wallace (1986), which found that the diet-plus-exercise group surprisingly did not lose as much weight as the diet-alone group. This appears to have been the result of compliance problems. The subjects in this dual treatment group simply failed to adhere to the treatment regimen.

If it is true that noncompliance is a major problem whenever active participation of the client is required, enhancing adherence to treatment regimens has got to be a major goal of health psychology. Moreover, behavioral management techniques should prove to be the treatment methods of choice. The efficacy of these procedures is illustrated through the published reports.

Several previously discussed research studies were aimed at improving adherence. Carney, Schechter, and Davis (1983) increased the frequency of blood glucose testing by a group of insulin-dependent diabetic children by consistently and systematically rewarding this behavior (see Figure 2.1). Dapcich-Miura and Hovel (1979) improved adherence to a complex medical regimen by an elderly heart patient with the use of a token economy (see Figure 4.2).

Thyer (1987b) promoted the use of seat belts by developing a contingency contract with the students in his course. Consequences involved what he referred to as "minor pedagogical incentives" (p. 166). That is, he raised a student's assignment grade to an A+ or reduced an assignment grade to an F if he observed a student either wearing or not wearing a seat belt, respectively. During the course of the semester, seat-belt usage rose significantly, from an average of 83.1 percent to 94.5 percent. (There was no report, however, about whether students took any further courses with this teacher.)

The importance of physical exercise as part of an overall weight-loss program has been previously discussed. Compliance can clearly be a major problem, but DeLuca and Holborn (1985) increased stationary bicycle riding by a group of fifth-grade boys who were 25 percent overweight. Reinforcers were chosen from one of Cautela's (1977) reinforcement surveys (see Chapter 2). The boys "were advised that they could earn points by exercising on the bicycle to 'buy' the items they liked best at the end of the exercise program" (p. 528).

Finally, Mayer, Dubbert, Scott, Dawson, Ekstrand, and Fondren (1987) improved the rate of breast self-examination (BSE) by an experimental group of women as compared to a control group. Although both groups had been taught how to conduct an examination and both received mail prompts to do so, the women in the experimental group also received a biweekly in-person "brief, discreet verbal reminder to practice BSE and verbal praise if the subject" had done so during the previous month (p. 139). Although overall compliance rates were still unfortunately low, there was a significant increase in BSE in the verbal-prompt-and-praise group.

Problems with compliance are again discussed in Chapter 7.

MANAGEMENT OF SPECIFIC DISORDERS

Pain

"Pain" is usually thought of as the result of a disease state, tissue damage, or the onset of some nociceptive stimulation. Although this view is correct, it is not complete. It doesn't go far enough. It fails to explain many instances of chronic pain for which no such stimulus appears to be present.

In the early 1970s, Wilbert Fordyce reconceptualized the view of chronic pain by reclassifying pain as either "respondent" or "operant." Respondent pain is the direct response to a specific organic stimulus. Operant pain, in contrast, may be learned, reinforced, and maintained through the rules of contingency management. That is, learned pain may be reinforced by its behavioral consequences in the patient's social environment.

Because pain cannot be directly observed, it is inferred through the presence of so-called "pain behaviors"—a variety of visible or audible behaviors made by the patient, including complaints, restriction of normal activities, and increased use of pain-controlling medications. Weisenberg (1983), in his chapter on pain control, describes the **Fordyce approach** and says that these pain behaviors exist "in an environment that had provided them with contingent reinforcement." They develop, he says, "as a consequence of pain behavior becoming contingent upon reinforcement. . . . Through reinforcement, pain behaviors may continue for reasons unrelated to the nociceptive tissue-damaging stimulus" (p. 100).

Some of the reinforcers that may induce operant pain or maintain pain behaviors include increased attention or sympathy from significant others; avoidance of unpleasant tasks, jobs, activities, or social relationships and responsibilities; money from disability compensation or impending litigation; and the positive, pleasant side effects of many pain-relieving medications. Clearly, both positive and negative reinforcement are at work. To illustrate the operant nature of some pain behaviors—I treated a patient whose chronic back pain (originally resulting from a serious fall) was frequently worse on days when her husband didn't have to go to work and was, therefore, available to perform various household responsibilities or simply sit with her, hold her hand, or talk. It is clear that "when the original respondent pain situation persists long enough under circumstances favorable to conditioning," operant pain may develop (Fordyce & Steger, 1979, p. 132).

Fordyce and Steger (1979) point out that "a basic principle of conditioning is that learning and conditioning effects are time-limited. An operant behavior established or conditioned will be maintained only as long as reinforcing contingencies are applied. The rate and magnitude of reinforcement may diminish, but if the positive consequence is completely halted, the operant behavior will eventually extinguish" (p. 133). This, then, becomes the focus of the Fordyce approach to pain management: Develop a program that reduces pain behaviors while simultaneously increasing a variety of incompatible "well behaviors." Well behaviors are many of the activities the patient would "normally" be involved in had the pain not developed in the first place. These include physical activity and a variety of both vocational and social pursuits.

To reduce pain behaviors (behavioral excesses) and increase well behaviors (behavioral deficits), the host of contingency management procedures previously described in this text can be employed. These include, but are not limited to, extinction, time-out, modeling and behavioral rehearsal, shaping, DRO, and contracting and token economy.

Because many patients with chronic pain have a long history of taking numerous pain-relieving medications and because many of these medications are capable of producing a pleasant "high" and are physically addictive, Fordyce acknowledges great potential for abuse. Any such medication administered on an as-needed (i.e., "prn") basis—contingent on the patient either asking for it or emitting some other pain behavior—may act as the reinforcer that increases the operant pain. Fordyce favors, instead, a program in which pain medication is administered on a time-dependent basis and the active ingredients are gradually phased out. Berni and Fordyce (1977) state, "When pain medications are put on a prn, or 'take only when needed,' basis, the result is that the patient's expressions of pain are systematically reinforced by receiving medications, and absence of pain is never reinforced by medications. . . . [This, therefore,] can serve as reinforcers to strengthen such pain behaviors as visible and audible signals of pain and asking for medications. In behavioral terms, pain medications, given on a prn basis, become pain contingent. Changing that arrangement so that medications become time contingent rather than pain contingent can help reduce both addiction or habituation and, in some instances, the pain itself" (pp. 147–148).

To illustrate an operant-based pain management program, Wright, Slucki, and Benetti (1983) treated a 10-year-old boy suffering from severe burns on his legs. At the time behavioral treatment was begun, the patient was uncooperative and oppositional during both medical and physical therapy treatments, was refusing to perform required exercises, had "picked off" several skin grafts, and frequently screamed and complained of pain. The result of the behavioral analysis indicated that his "screaming, complaints of pain and opposition to treatment were frequently consequated by increased attention from those individuals present during treatment" (p. 34). These observations suggested to the authors that if they eliminated these consequences by differentially reinforcing compliance with the physical therapy program, positive behavior change might result.

Behavioral treatment, therefore, involved the use of extensive verbal praise for the boy's compliance with various aspects of the physical therapy program and for even brief episodes of nonpain behaviors (DRO and shaping components). While attention was thus given for cooperation, crying and complaining were extinguished. Results were dramatic: Pain behaviors decreased, well behaviors increased, and the boy was discharged from the hospital after 14 days. Follow-up two and one-half years later indicated that his legs had healed, his functional level was normal, and he suffered no other somatic complaints.

Hypertension

The Joint National Committee on Detection, Evaluation, and Treatment of High Blood Pressure (1984) estimated that more than 60 million Americans have elevated blood pressure (BP). Although there are some specific physiological causes of high blood pressure, in approximately 80 percent of the cases—referred to as "essential hypertension"—no such cause can be determined.

Antihypertensive medication can clearly be effective in the treatment of many cases of high BP, but because of a variety of contraindications or side effects of these drugs, nonpharmacological treatments are gaining in popularity. These include weight reduction; restriction in the consumption of dietary sodium, alcohol, and fats; cessation of smoking; increase of regular physical exercise; and stress management or relaxation and biofeedback therapies.

As should by now be readily apparent, all these treatments fall within the realm of health psychology, and various behavioral procedures should, therefore, be helpful in their modification. The Joint National Committee's (1984) report states that "behavioral methods in hypertension management . . . may consistently produce modest, but substantial, BP reduction" and that "therefore, behavioral therapy should be considered in the context of a comprehensive treatment program that may include both pharmacologic and nonpharmacologic therapeutic approaches" (p. 1048).

The report also speaks favorably about the use of **relaxation and biofeedback therapies**. Not limited to the treatment of high blood pressure, biofeedback is frequently a part of many other health psychology interventions. For the purposes of enhancing relaxation—and, thus, reducing stress—it can be found in cessation of smoking, weight-control, and pain management programs. The next section focuses on the definition and wide application of biofeedback training.

BIOFEEDBACK

Although not traditionally considered an aspect of behavior modification or contingency management, the operant conditioning paradigm is considered by a number of authors to form the basis for biofeedback training as well. Schwartz and Beatty (1977) define biofeedback as a "group of experimental procedures in which an external sensor is used to provide the organism with an indication of the state of a bodily process, usually in an attempt to effect a change in the measured quantity. That indication has been termed 'feedback' (hence, biofeedback) or 'reinforcement' " (p. 1). Lubar and Shouse (1977) define biofeedback as a "methodology for acquiring learned control over internal processes. Essentially, biofeedback is operant conditioning of autonomic, electrophysiological, and neuromuscular responses. The procedure usually involves making an exteroceptive stimulus contingent upon some clearly delineated change of an internal response, resulting in control of the targeted response" (p. 204). Additionally, Miller (1985) states that a "Key element in the development of biofeedback was the idea that instrumental learning (i.e., operant conditioning) reinforced by rewards and punishments could modify a wider range of responses—visceral ones, brain waves, and those involved in certain neuromuscular disorders—than hitherto had been believed to be possible" (pp. 11–12). (See Miller, 1969, for an excellent review of the early history of biofeedback.)

To illustrate, a patient's autonomic or central nervous system response, such as heart rate, is monitored. If decreases in this biological process are reinforced, those changes tend to recur and the heart rate goes down. With human subjects, actual reinforcement may not be necessary. Appropriate changes in the target response can be fed back to the client by means of a dial, numerical display, light, tone, and so on that fluctuates with the biological process and provides knowledge of results. According to Shapiro and Surwit (1979), "informational and reinforcing properties are both involved in the biofeedback stimuli and procedure. Thus, aside from its reinforcing properties, the reinforcer itself may also be informational, indicating to the subject that the desired response has occurred. Aside from its informational characteristics, the biofeedback stimulus may be reinforcing, indicating to the subject that he or she has done the right thing, has achieved the desired result, or has been successful in the task" (p. 46). Olton and Noonberg (1980) similarly describe the feedback stimulus as a secondary reinforcer. Although it has no intrinsic value, it gains its reinforcing characteristics from its relationship to the successful change in the biological process.

Olton and Noonberg (1980) further describe the feedback process as a control loop (see Figure 5.1). "The patient attempts to control heart rate, heart rate changes in some fashion, information about the actual heart rate change is provided, the patient evaluates the outcome, makes changes in his attempt to control heart rate, observes the subsequent results, makes further changes, and so on" (p. 12). Using this procedure, clients can be taught to control a wide variety of autonomic and central nervous system responses. In fact, it may be that any labile biological response—if it can be monitored and if information regarding changes can be fed back to the client—can be brought under such operant control.

In clinical and research settings, biofeedback has been used to teach

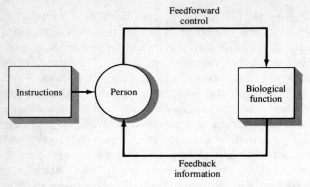

Figure 5.1 Biofeedback indicated as a general control process. (*Source:* D. S. Olton and A. R. Noonberg, *Biofeedback: Clinical Applications in Behavioral Medicine* [Englewood Cliffs, N.J.: Prentice-Hall, 1980]. Copyright 1980 by Prentice-Hall, Inc. Reprinted by permission of the publisher.)

control of such response systems as the cardiovascular, muscular, and electroencephalographic. Problems treated include hypertension, hypotension, insomnia, colitis, Reynaud's syndrome, temperomandibular joint (TMJ) distress, muscle tension and migraine headaches, premature ventricular contractions, tachycardia, epilepsy, hyperactivity, penile erection, and vaginismus. The most commonly employed pieces of biofeedback equipment include the electromyograph (EMG) to monitor and feed back information regarding muscle activity, the electroencephalograph (EEG) for brain wave activity, skin temperature (thermal) recorders to monitor blood volume indirectly, electrodermal response (EDR) recorders for electrical activity and resistance of the skin (also referred to as the galvanic skin response—GSR), and blood pressure and heart rate monitoring devices.

An illustration of a "typical" biofeedback study is that by Blanchard, McCoy, Musso, Gerardi, Pallmeyer, Gerardi, Cotch, Siracusa, and Andrasik (1986), who treated patients suffering from high blood pressure. Before the study, these patients had been treated for an average of more than eight years with at least two simultaneous antihypertensive medications. The new treatment consisted of thermal (hand-warming) biofeedback. Patients received twice-weekly, 60-minute biofeedback training sessions for eight weeks along with considerable home practice. The major dependent variable was the ability of the patient to be adequately maintained on only one antihypertensive medication. Long-term follow-up (one year) found that significantly more biofeedback patients were still using only one drug as compared to the control group.

Although the target problems amenable to treatment with biofeedback differ greatly from those discussed in earlier chapters of this text, they can all be viewed as examples of behavioral excesses and deficits. Furthermore, Black, Cott, and Pavloski (1977), in their chapter "The Operant Learning Theory Approach to Biofeedback Training," show that such typical contingency management processes as reinforcement, shaping, and stimulus-discrimination training have been demonstrated in biofeedback. The responses being controlled and the equipment being used may certainly differ, but the principles are very much the same.

Although there is some controversy regarding the efficacy of biofeedback therapy (see, e.g., Miller, 1985; Roberts, 1985), Noonberg (1985) found that 58 percent of the psychology graduate programs surveyed are presently offering some training in biofeedback to their students.

To summarize, the principles and procedures of behavior modification clearly have applications in medical settings—just as they have previously been demonstrated in psychological clinics, schools, and the home.

Chapter 6

Implementing the Interventions: Much to Consider

RATIONALE PRESENTED TO CLIENT AND THE THERAPEUTIC ENVIRONMENT

Behavior modification as an organized profession has always been both sensitive and responsive to the criticism that likens it to a totalitarian, Orwellian method of mind control. The public's misconception is well illustrated in an article by Turkat and Feuerstein (1978), who found that over a several-year period, nearly half of the articles in *The New York Times* dealing with behavior modification likened it to brainwashing, sensory deprivation, Chinese water torture, psychosurgery, and the use of drugs.

In response to these types of criticisms, the Association for Advancement of Behavior Therapy (AABT) published a set of ethical guidelines (1977) that stressed open and free communication between the therapist and client (see Table 6.1). The tone of these guidelines is epitomized by the first two, which pose the questions "Have the therapist and client agreed on the goals of therapy?" and "Has the client's understanding of the goals been assured . . . ?" The feeling is one of a collaborative effort between the parties involved, with everything explained and nothing left hidden or secret.

Even beyond the ethical consideration, making treatment plans as clear as possible and treatment goals explicit have empirical therapeutic value. Seidner and Kirschenbaum (1980) found that clients who received information about treatment strategy and expected outcomes showed both enhanced involvement, as measured by attitudes in interviews and

Table 6.1 ETHICAL ISSUES FOR HUMAN SERVICES

A. Have the goals of treatment been adequately considered?
   1. To ensure that the goals are explicit, are they written?
   2. Has the client's understanding of the goals been assured by having the client restate them orally or in writing?
   3. Have the therapist and client agreed on the goals of therapy?
   4. Will serving the client's interests be contrary to the interests of other persons?
   5. Will serving the client's immediate interests be contrary to the client's long-term interests?

B. Has the choice of treatment methods been adequately considered?
   1. Does the published literature show the procedure to be the best one available for that problem?
   2. If no literature exists regarding the treatment method, is the method consistent with generally accepted practice?
   3. Has the client been told of alternative procedures that might be preferred by the client on the basis of significant differences in discomfort, treatment time, cost, or degree of demonstrated effectiveness?
   4. If a treatment procedure is publicly, legally, or professionally controversial, has formal professional consultation been obtained, has the reaction of the affected segment of the public been adequately considered, and have the alternative treatment methods been more closely reexamined and reconsidered?

C. Is the client's participation voluntary?
   1. Have possible sources of coercion on the client's participation been considered?
   2. If treatment is legally mandated, has the available range of treatments and therapists been offered?
   3. Can the client withdraw from treatment without a penalty or financial loss that exceeds actual clinical costs?

D. When another person or an agency is empowered to arrange for therapy, have the interests of the subordinated client been sufficiently considered?
   1. Has the subordinated client been informed of the treatment objectives and participated in the choice of treatment procedures?
   2. Where the subordinated client's competence to decide is limited, has the client as well as the guardian participated in the treatment discussion to the extent that the client's abilities permit?
   3. If the interests of the subordinated person and the superordinate persons or agency conflict, have attempts been made to reduce the conflict by dealing with both interests?

E. Has the adequacy of treatment been evaluated?
   1. Have quantitative measures of the problem and its progress been obtained?
   2. Have the measures of the problem and its progress been made available to the client during treatment?

F. Has the confidentiality of the treatment relationship been protected?
   1. Has the client been told who has access to the records?
   2. Are records available only to authorized persons?

Table 6.1 (*Continued*)

G. Does the therapist refer the clients to other therapists when necessary?
   1. If treatment is unsuccessful, is the client referred to other therapists?
   2. Has the client been told that, if dissatisfied with the treatment, referral will be made?

H. Is the therapist qualified to provide treatment?
   1. Has the therapist had training or experience in treating problems like the client's?
   2. If deficits exist in the therapist's qualifications, has the client been informed?
   3. If the therapist is not adequately qualified, is the client referred to other therapists, or has supervision by a qualified therapist been provided? Is the client informed of the supervisory relation?
   4. If the treatment is administered by mediators, have the mediators been adequately supervised by a qualified therapist?

Source: Association for Advancement of Behavior Therapy, Ethical issues for human services, *Behavior Therapy, 8* (1977), 763–764. Copyright 1977 by the Association for Advancement of Behavior Therapy. Reprinted by permission of the publisher.

work toward assignments, and more obvious and positive behavior changes as compared to control groups not receiving such information. The authors concluded that "these findings suggest that one of the key elements of behavioral contracts is their specification of treatment strategies or plans" (p. 697).

Obviously, the degree to which clients can be involved in planning treatment strategy varies with their competencies. Young children, the retarded, the psychotic, and the senile may have capabilities too diminished for them to become involved in the planning process. However, the AABT guidelines still call for their participation to the extent that their abilities permit, as well as the participation of their responsible agents.

In addition to an a priori collaborative effort in the planning of an intervention, its degree of effectiveness frequently depends on the extent to which contingencies are made clear during implementation. Although verbalization of the contingency is not essential, as shown by the success of operant conditioning with nonhumans, one usually states the contingency to the client. That is, when a positive reinforcer is contingent on the emission of a target behavioral deficit, a phrase such as "This is because . . ." reinforces the if-then character of the contract involved. Moreover, other statements used concurrently (e.g., "That's good!") can become powerful social reinforcers, capable themselves of maintaining behavior changes.

In sum, Bellack and Hersen (1977) state that "whenever possible, clients are provided with complete, accurate information about the (behavioral) rationale for treatment as well as its course, cost, and the prognosis *before* entering into any *voluntary* agreement to accept treatment" (p. 22).

Therapeutic Environment

The term *therapeutic environment* has two distinct meanings: the setting in which behavior modification takes place and the relationship between the therapist and the client. As the literature previously cited illustrates, contingency management has been effectively used in a wide range of settings, with no one site consistently shown to be more effective or successful. The various settings do differ, however, with respect to the amount of control the therapist has over the client's behavior and its consequences and the consistency with which an intervention can be administered. These variables do influence the efficiency of the contingency management program.

In terms of the therapist-client environment, the atmosphere of openness and collaboration has already been discussed. Bellack and Hersen (1977) use this atmosphere to counter the claim that behavior therapists, because of the emphasis placed on objectivity, explicitness, and empiricism, are cold, insensitive, callous, and impersonal. They refer to a study by Sloane, Staples, Cristol, Yorkston, and Whipple (1975) that found that "clients rated behavior therapists at least as high on interpersonal factors such as warmth and empathy as non-behavioral therapists" (Bellack & Hersen, p. 22). They stress that although the "client-therapist relationship is not the source of change . . . a positive relationship is desirable in therapy, and that it is often a necessary but not sufficient factor in generating change" (p. 22).

In an interesting counterposition to that expressed by Bellack and Hersen, Turkat and Brantley (1981) state that although the most common approach to the therapist-client relationship is probably that of providing a warm, supportive, empathetic environment, they feel that there is a minimum of evidence to support its efficacy. Therefore, it might not be the most appropriate approach for all clients. Basing their argument on the empirical nature of behavior therapy, they feel that "each case presents unique independent and dependent variable relationships, [and that] treatment must, therefore, be individually tailored to fit the specific . . . variables isolated for each client. . . . It would seem illogical to expect that a single mode of therapist-client interaction would be optimal for promoting change in all cases. Thus, to assume that a warm, empathetic and supportive environment is an efficacious independent variable in every case is to ignore individual differences" (p. 16). They then give several examples of varying the therapeutic relationship in accordance with the client's behavior. One such example involves making the therapist's verbal approval contingent on the performance of certain target behaviors by a schizophrenic patient.

Bornstein and Rychtarik (1983) reviewed the literature regarding consumer satisfaction with behavior therapy and other therapeutic approaches and the acceptability of various behavioral treatment procedures. In summary, they concluded that "no study was found in which the behavioral approach was less satisfactory or less favored. Thus, it appears that behavioral procedures are just as viable, if not more so, when consumer satisfaction variables are taken into account" (pp. 194–195).

Client Variables

As the literature previously cited in this text illustrates, behavior modification has been effectively utilized with as wide a range of clients as possible: from children only several months old to the elderly, from those with normal intelligence to the profoundly retarded, from those otherwise healthy to those medically ill, and from those with minor behavior problems to those with severe psychoses. No one group or client variable has been shown to be universally more amenable or better suited to the procedures described in this text.

Although the basic principles of behavior modification remain the same, each implementation must be attuned to the particular clients involved and their specific characteristics and needs. Obviously, clients differ in their ability to become (and interest in becoming) active participants in the development of treatment strategies and goals. As previously discussed, clients also differ with respect to what will act as effective positive reinforcers. Particular client populations present special problems. With the client who lives alone, there may be difficulty obtaining independent verification of client-assessed behaviors. A significant other to act as change agent may also be absent. With these clients there is even greater need to explain the procedures and their rationale. Additionally, the client can be taught to administer contingent consequences. Mentally retarded clients don't always understand instructions and, therefore, don't always implement a procedure correctly. Additional time to ensure understanding may be required. The utilization of paraprofessional agents of the therapist who make home visits can also help with both of these client populations. Although client-related problems can affect the implementation and efficiency of an intervention, they do not nullify the usefulness of behavior modification.

EQUIPMENT

With the exception of some highly sophisticated equipment used in an occasional study (e.g., Heller & Strang, 1973, who automatically monitored teeth grinding frequency and delivered an aversive sound blast through a speaker in the client's ear; or Greene, Bailey, & Barber, 1981, whose automatic sound-recording device measured duration and frequency of outbursts on a school bus), the vast majority of behavior modification interventions use a minimum amount of equipment. Because behavior and behavior change are described in terms of their measurable characteristics, most of the equipment is used to measure duration, frequency, and intensity. Duration and frequency are measured simply with timers and counters. Fimian (1980), in a technical report, describes what he calls "an inexpensive, homemade, and compact table-top device for easily obtaining concurrent duration and frequency measures" (p. 22). It contains two stopwatches and a golf counter. As a further example, one equipment company (Lehigh Valley Electronics) manufactures a "classroom control points counter," a display unit with a three-digit readout and a hand-held actuator. With this device, a teacher, for example, can register points (tokens) for various behaviors by remote control.

The intensity of a behavior is somewhat more difficult to measure, in that the equipment required is more sophisticated. Lehigh Valley Electronics, again as an illustration, markets a "classroom control noise monitor." As classroom noise rises above a level preset by the teacher, the class loses accumulated points because the counter automatically resets. This apparatus, then, is a programmed decibel meter. As illustrated, equipment is used not only to quantify behavior but also to consequate it. There are automatic positive reinforcer (e.g., candy, marbles) dispensers as well as remote-controlled and hand-held (self-administered) shockers (negative reinforcer dispensers).

As an example of perhaps the most elaborate use of equipment, Elwood (1975) describes a fully automated clinical service center. This "Automated Psychology Laboratory" is equipped with closed-circuit cameras, speakers and microphones, computers, tape players, client response panels, physiological recording devices, and slide and film projectors. They are programmed to provide "responsive" or "interactive" clinical services, including interviewing, testing, and remediation, without a "live" therapist.

In addition, sophisticated equipment is required in a biofeedback procedure to monitor and provide information regarding various physiological processes. The most commonly used pieces of biofeedback equipment include the electromyograph (EMG), the electroencephalograph (EEG), skin temperature recorders, electrodermal response (EDR) recorders, and blood pressure and heart rate monitoring devices.

Although paper-and-pencil inventories, charts, tables, graphs, and other data-gathering devices are perhaps not technically referred to as equipment, behavior modification does rely heavily on the use of a variety of these items.

DATA GATHERING

Contrary to Martin and Pear's (1983) facetious statement "Data! Data! Data! Why bother?" (p. 294), data gathering in behavior modification serves at least four major functions. First (not necessarily in order of importance), data gathering allows the therapist to determine if the intervention is working. If one views a therapeutic intervention as a mini-experiment, a baselevel-intervention-postintervention comparison provides the empirical evidence required to determine its efficacy and to decide whether any procedural alterations are necessary. Moreover, it is often difficult, especially in the early stages of an intervention, to tell if any change is occurring without some factual material for comparison. Just as it is frequently impossible to use a voice vote to decide a majority position, examining a behavioral situation "by eye or ear" can be similarly inconclusive. This is more frequently the case when the behavior change, to borrow from the field of psychophysics, is less than a just noticeable difference (jnd). Think of a 300-pound client who attempts a weight-loss program. During the first week the client loses 2 pounds, and during the second week an additional 3 pounds. If this client did not collect data (i.e., weigh and record the weights), the admirable 5-pound loss—constituting, however, a mere 1.7 percent—might be below the difference threshold and, therefore, not noticed. This lack could well result in discouragement and the premature termination of the program. Similarly, a teacher or parent might not "notice" a reduction of two or three disruptive outbursts, especially if they constituted a small percentage change, during the first few days of extinguishing a behavioral excess. Without a graph documenting the behavior change, the intervention might be thought to be not working.

To test the efficacy of a behavioral intervention, an **A–B–A–B reversal design** is frequently used. *A* is the baselevel condition without the intervention; *B* is the intervention or treatment phase. If the client's behavior changes each time the therapist changes the contingencies, the consequences are said to have affected the changes in the behavior. For example, Dapcich-Miura and Hovell (1979), in a previously discussed study, used contingency management to improve an elderly heart patient's adherence to a complex medical regimen. Tokens were earned for taking walks, drinking orange juice, and taking medication. As Figure 4.2 indicates, during baselevel (A) the frequency of each of the target behaviors was quite low (behavioral deficit). Each rose to approximately 300 percent above baselevel during the token phase (B), dropped again during the second baselevel (A), and once again rose when the contingency was reinstated (B). The fact that the behavior mirrored the contingencies shows the effectiveness of the intervention. The A–B–A–B reversal design is, perhaps, the most common efficacy test found in the behavioral literature.

A potential ethical problem arises, however, with use of this design: Once treatment has produced a desired effect on behavior, should the therapist cause it to revert to baselevel? Two of the possible solutions to this dilemma that still provide data on treatment efficacy are multiple-baseline designs and multiple-group designs.

In a **multiple-baseline design**, the therapist monitors two or more behaviors concurrently but implements intervention at different times. If behavior 1 changes only when its intervention begins, and if behavior 2 changes only when its intervention begins, the behavior change is said to be caused by the intervention. The Dapcich-Miura and Hovell (1979) study (see Figure 4.2) is also an example of such a multiple-baseline design. The token reinforcement phase (B) for each of the three target behaviors was begun at a different time (see the first vertical broken line). It should be noted that each target behavior, in turn, only increased in frequency when its contingency management program was begun. This result, again, validates the effectiveness of the procedure.

With a **multiple-group design**, two or more matched groups or individuals are monitored through baselevel and then intervention is begun in only one of the groups. With all other factors held constant, if behavior changes only in the intervention group, a causal relationship is concluded and efficacy is determined.

The second function of data gathering is that it helps determine whether the problem is, in fact, one worthy of remediation. A staff member working in an institution for the retarded observed one of the residents eating a cigarette butt. It was immediately decided that this was an excess to be eliminated. Baselevel data collection, however, indicated that this response was not emitted again during the next seven days, and the case was closed. A female client receiving marital therapy told the therapist that her husband spent an excessive amount of time in the bathroom and that this was one of their problems. After a week of timing his bathroom behavior, she reported that she was surprised that it wasn't as much time as she had thought, and she now wanted to go on to another problem.

The third function of data gathering is that it can have actual therapeutic value in that it often affects the behavior being monitored. Redd and Sleator (1976) give the example of a teacher who was having difficulty with disruptive classroom behaviors by a number of children. She was instructed in the use of DRO and asked to self-monitor, as baselevel, the number of times she reinforced cooperative behaviors. The data indicated that she began to show a steady increase in these behaviors over the next several days (although this was not the instruction), with a corresponding reduction of disruptions.

The fourth function of data gathering is that it helps determine the specific intervention of choice. That is, the data gathered lead to the differential diagnosis, which, in turn, should signify the appropriate treatment strategy. Edelson, Taubman, and Lovaas (1983) illustrate this process with the life-threatening and self-destructive behaviors often seen in some autistic and mentally retarded individuals. Such self-injurious behaviors (SIB) as body pinching, hand biting, and head banging could be under the control of at least three processes. (1) The SIB could be "instrumental social behavior, shaped and maintained by contingent positive reinforcement" (p. 300). That is, it could get attention, reinforced by increased staff contact. If this were the case, effective treatment might involve extinction and DRO (staff attention for non-SIB). (2) An "individual [might] respond with self-abuse to escape, avoid, or terminate an aversive stimulus or situation, such as a caretaker's demand" (p. 300). That is, the SIB might be negatively reinforced by the withdrawal of a demand placed on the individual. If this were the case, effective treatment might involve teaching both patient tolerance for demands as well as staff persistence. (3) An "individual [might] engage in self-injury to obtain sensory feedback or arousal from the behavior itself; thus, the individual is seen as dependent on self-abuse to provide his or her own sensory reinforcement" (p. 300). That is, the SIB might be positively reinforced by the sensory arousal or stimulation it provides (sensory-reinforcement theory). If this were the case, effective treatment might involve sensory extinction and DRO (arousing stimulation for non-SIB). Edelson, Taubman, and Lovaas conclude that since the intervention evolves from the analysis of the contingencies involved, these conditions associated with the SIB must be considered in the formulation of the treatment program.

Meredith and Milby (1980) also describe four general objectives of behavioral assessment. They are (1) "to provide a detailed, objective definition of the behavioral problems"; (2) "to devise behavioral objectives and . . . intervention program"; (3) "to develop an ongoing objective evaluation of treatment"; and (4) to increase "motivation for change via specification of problems, communication of understanding, and increasing expectancy of change" (pp. 31–32).

Once it is determined that data gathering is important, how is it accomplished? Wade, Baker, and Hartmann (1979), in their survey of 257 AABT members, asked respondents to indicate the assessment techniques they employed. The three most frequently used techniques were behavioral interviews (76.3 percent of therapists with 53.8 percent of clients), behavioral observation (70.4 percent of therapists with 33.9 percent of clients), and behavioral surveys (49.4 percent of therapists with 20.3 percent of clients). Data gathering can further be divided into the following five categories: self-report, observation, self-monitoring, permanent-product measures, and physiological measures.

Self-Report

Self-report is essentially the technique used in behavioral interviews and surveys. Although perhaps the most commonly used technique, it has certain disadvantages. Because behavior is not directly observed, but is instead inferred through verbal reports, distortion and inaccuracy are inevitable, raising questions of validity and reliability. Clients may talk about their subjective impressions of their behaviors, but not about quantifiable characteristics. However, self-report, problems notwithstanding, has convenience as its major advantage.

Both to save time and to help focus a client's responses, numerous self-report surveys or questionnaires are available. These can measure mood, pinpoint what stimuli evoke fear or anxiety, determine the physiological response to stress, delineate assertive behavior and interaction problems, and assess sexual orientation. (See Cautela, 1977, 1981.)

Observation

The three major direct behavior observation techniques are event recording, interval recording (time sampling), and duration recording. **Event recording** involves "direct observation and recording of discrete responses . . . in which an observer records each occurrence of a target behavior during some specified period of time in order to establish its frequency" (Bellack & Hersen, 1977, p. 26). Because event recording involves the observation of *every* occurrence of the response, the procedure is somewhat more cumbersome than **interval recording**. Here, "each observation period is subdivided into brief intervals (15–30 seconds is common), and the observer simply records whether or not (not how many times) the target response occurs during that interval" (p. 27). **Duration recording** involves a measurement of the length of time a target behavior occurs. Using "telephone behavior" as an illustration, event recording might record the number of phone calls made per day, interval recording might record whether or not a call was being made during each time interval sampled, and duration recording might record the length of phone calls. Although several studies (e.g., Murphy & Goodall, 1980; Smith, Madsen, & Cipani, 1981) compare various observation techniques and various intervals within time sampling, no one technique or time interval consistently produces more reliable data than any other. One must "simply" choose the technique that best seems to fit the situation at hand.

A–B–C Analysis   As part of a behavioral assessment, the observer might perform an **A–B–C analysis**. In such an observation, *A* represents the *a*ntecedents of the target behavior, *B* represents the *b*ehavior itself, and *C* represents the *c*onsequences of the behavior. By observing the patterns of stimulus events prior to the maladaptive target behavior and what consistently happens to the environment or client after it is made, one often gets a better picture of the various conditions controlling that behavior. An A–B–C analysis frequently helps determine whether the target behavior is a respondent (i.e., evoked by an environmental stimulus) and/ or an operant (i.e., maintained by its consequences). This determination is prescriptive because it frequently leads to the appropriate intervention strategy. Contingency management is most effective when the behavior is an operant. I treated a mildly retarded adolescent, "George," with the bizarre behavioral excess of biting his left thumb (see Case Study, Chapter 4). An A–B–C analysis revealed that he emitted this behavior (B) in the presence of his mother when she told him that he couldn't do something or go someplace he wanted to (A). As a consequence of his behavior, she frequently gave in (C). Treatment involved simultaneously teaching him (DRO) more appropriate ways of dealing with frustration (his behavioral deficit) while teaching his mother to extinguish his biting (behavioral excess).

Although observations can be made by the therapist, because of various time and financial constraints, they are more often made by someone else. The observer is frequently an associate or technician trained by the therapist (possibly a student or staff member or teacher in a hospital or school) or a significant other in the client's home (parent, spouse). Since accurate observation and recording of data are time-consuming and often viewed as a burden or a chore, Hollander and Plutchik (1972) used a token economy to increase these behaviors by psychiatric hospital attendants. Observations, in addition, are frequently made by the client himself or herself.

Self-Monitoring

Self-monitoring, according to Haynes (1978), "has been used as an assessment or intervention instrument with a wide range of target behaviors and populations" (p. 294), including children, retardates, and institutionalized individuals. He believes that "any response which can be identified, observed, and recorded by the client is apparently amenable to assessment through self-monitoring" (p. 296).

The major *advantages* of self-monitoring are apparent when the responses to be observed are either infrequent, private, or covert. Because of cost and/or convenience factors, it is, in practice, prohibitive to use trained professionals to observe such low-rate behaviors as occasional alcoholic binges, episodes of exhibitionism, and arguments with the boss. With private behaviors (e.g., sexual) and covert behaviors (e.g., headaches, nightmares, and suicidal thoughts), a process in which the client does the observing and recording may be the best or only technique available.

The two major *disadvantages* of self-monitoring are interrelated. First, as previously mentioned, self-monitoring frequently affects the behavior being observed. That is, the process is "reactive" and, therefore, brings the validity and the utility of the observation into question. Second, self-monitored behavior may lack objectivity. Do data derived from self-observation accurately reflect the behavior under question? How do self-observation data correlate with "nonreactive" observations by others? The lower the correlation, the less the validity. Haynes (1978) believes that the therapist can increase the accuracy of self-monitoring data "if time is taken to insure that the subject can identify the target behavior, understands the recording methods, and comprehends the importance of reliable and accurate tracking" (p. 297). In addition, contingent positive reinforcement for accurate data collection can be effectively employed.

Permanent Product Measures

Permanent product measures of data gathering, according to Bellack and Hersen (1977) entail "the observation of the effects or products of a response. The presence of the product *infers* that a specific response occurred" (p. 25). They provide, for example, results on an exam as the product from which to infer that a student had studied and learned, and washed dishes as the product from which to infer that someone had cleaned up. Such measures are most useful when direct observation of the behavior, for a variety of reasons, is not feasible, as with, for example, encopresis or enuresis. However, because the behavior is not directly observed, but only inferred, occasional errors are made. Good grades on an exam do not necessarily mean that the student has studied, just as a good dental checkup does not necessarily mean that a preventive-care regimen has been followed. Moreover, permanent product measures, again because the behavior is not directly observed, involve a certain loss of information about specific characteristics of the behavior—for example, intensity or duration. To use the same example, a good grade on an exam could result from 15 minutes of casual review or 3 hours of intensive study.

Physiological Measures

Physiological measures of assessment—for example, the recording of the activity of the autonomic nervous system—have found considerable applicability in behavior therapy, especially in biofeedback. Such physiological responses as muscle activity (EMG), brain wave patterns (EEG), electrodermal response (EDR, GSR), skin temperature, heart rate and blood pressure, intestinal motility, penile erection, vaginal blood flow, and so on have been monitored and recorded for both assessment and remediation. Physiological measures, however, have limited usefulness in other aspects of contingency management.

RECORD KEEPING

Although it is within the session when the client-therapist relationship is established, interviewing and initial assessment take place, data previously collected are reviewed, and rationale of treatment is planned and discussed, there is a minimum amount of specific *within-session* contingency management record keeping. The exception involves biofeedback, in which a target physiological response is monitored and information fed back to the client so that a change in that response can be learned.

Almost all the data collected in contingency management involve one or more of the quantifiable characteristics of behavior and constitute *between-session* record keeping. Once instructed in the appropriate data-gathering technique, and once the behavior to be observed is clearly defined, the observer can record the data in a variety of ways. However, a simple table and/or graph—with, for example, daily tally entries—is usually sufficient. This method provides both the actual data plus a visual representation of behavior change. This is by far the most common form of record keeping in the literature.

Several sources (e.g., Cautela, 1977, 1981; Walker & Shea, 1980) provide a number of specific forms to be used for record keeping. Walker and Shea's behavior modification text is designed for educators and includes an appendix containing five perforated copies of each worksheet and form discussed in the text. These forms include, among others, a "point card" (with spaces for the child's name and date and number, representing a running total number of points, ranging from 1 to 100), a "point tally form" (with spaces to log in the number of points earned on each day of the week), a "time-out log" (with columns for the time the child enters time-out; leaves time-out; and behavior before, during, and after time-out), and a "behavior log form" (with columns for the antecedents and consequences of a given behavior during a specific time period).

Cautela's books are spiral-bound compilations of behavior analysis forms that can be removed and reproduced freely. These forms include various "reinforcement survey schedules"—to help determine potential positive reinforcers for a number of different client populations—and a "weekly record of reinforcing events," in which clients log (with time, place, and date) any event they find pleasant or enjoyable. Again, this form is helpful in the determination of positive reinforcers as well as the assessment of client activity. Cautela's 1981 book also includes a "weekly homework record," an "assertive behavior record," and "guidelines" for both parental discipline and time-out. Many of the record-keeping forms are to be filled out by the client as "homework."

HOMEWORK

Shelton and Levy (1981) surveyed the reported use of assigned homework activities in eight behavior therapy journals over the past six years. Working under the assumption that efficiency of behavior change "comes from putting clients to work during the other 167 hours of the week not devoted to formal therapy" (p. 13), they found that 60 percent of the 330 treatments reviewed used home or outside practice assignments. Unfortunately, only 15 percent of the articles discussed how frequently the client should practice, only 11 percent discussed duration of practice, and a mere 7 percent even mentioned homework compliance rates.

What does the client do as homework? These assignments tend to fall into one of two categories: assessment and intervention (remediation). During the assessment phase, the client might be instructed to collect baselevel data on the frequency, duration, and/or intensity of the target behavior; record the conditions (time, place, and activity) in which the behavior occurs, its antecedents, and its consequences; and locate potential positive reinforcers. During the intervention phase, the client is to implement the program collaboratively developed with the therapist as well as continue to gather data regarding the behavior for comparison purposes. Record keeping for the client can be in the form of tables, graphs, diaries, logs, and so on.

GROUP ADMINISTRATION

Although Rimm and Masters (1979) state as one of the basic tenets of behavior therapy that the therapist individualizes, or "adapts his method of treatment to the client's problem" (p. 10), contingency management is frequently administered in a group setting, where a number of clients have similar problems.

Probably the first published report of treating a group as a single responding organism with contingency management is that by Schmidt and Ulrich (1969). In one of their experiments, "group control procedures were designed to suppress excessive classroom sound. The class was allowed a 2-minute addition to the gym period and a 2-minute break contingent upon maintaining an unbroken 10-minute quiet period as monitored on a decibel meter" (p. 171). If the decibel (dB) level in the classroom remained below an arbitrarily chosen 42 for each entire monitoring period, the whole class received a positive reinforcer. If at any time during the ten-minute period the dB level rose above 42, a signal was sounded and the ten-minute clock was reset. The data indicate a dramatic and sudden reduction in noise level when the group contingency was implemented.

Speltz, Moore, and McReynolds (1979) report that in recent years, group contingency management has become more complex, "providing for the reward of all or part of a group depending on the behavior of all or part of that group" (p. 219). Their study was designed to test the efficacy of a variety of group administration procedures. Subjects were 54 students in an introductory psychology course. The target behavior was the submission of multiple-choice questions presumably to be included in the test item pool. Reinforcement was extra credit to be added to the final grades. Students were divided into one of five treatment conditions: (1) "request only"—merely asked to submit questions; (2) "free reward"—asked to submit questions and given noncontingent extra credit points; (3) "standardized contingency"—individualized contingency in which only the students handing in questions received points; (4) "interdependent-responders"—if at least 8 of the 12 students handed in questions, those doing so would receive points; and (5) "interdependent-all-member"—if at least 8 of the 12 students handed in questions, all students would receive points.

The researchers found that "the results are unambiguous in their support of the use of interdependent group contingencies in the present applied context" (p. 225). Both interdependent contingent groups (4 and 5) showed a higher rate of response than did the widely used standardized contingency group (3), which, in turn, was superior to the two control groups (1 and 2). The group with the highest overall response rate was the interdependent-responder group (4), providing an interdependent contingency but with reward only for responders. The authors conclude that "there is, in sum, much to recommend the use of group operant contingencies in applied behavior-change settings" (p. 226).

Roberts and Fanurik (1986) developed a relatively simple group contingency program to increase the use of seat belts. They observed all cars delivering children to an elementary school between 7:30 and 8:15 A.M. After the initial baselevel phase, if *all* the occupants of the car (including the adult driver) were wearing seat belts, a variety of rewards were administered. These included colored bumper stickers, coloring books, and lottery tickets good for a free pizza. Also included was a pizza party for the class with the highest compliance rate. Seat-belt usage rose from 4.3 percent during baselevel to 66.2 percent during the four-week group contingency reinforcement phase.

Rose, in his two books on behavioral group therapy (1977, 1980), delineates the applicability of behavioral interventions in a group situation. In most cases, "clients are taught within the group to generate new and more effective behaviors in situations where they had previously experienced stress or inadequacy. They are taught to discriminate among situations calling for different types of behavior. . . . The group is considered both the context and vehicle of individual behavior change" (1977, pp. ix–x). Various chapters in these books deal with such procedures as contracting, behavioral rehearsal, parent training, communication and social skills training, and weight control. The applicability of behavioral group therapy was demonstrated in diverse populations and settings.

PARAPROFESSIONAL ADMINISTRATION AND SELF-HELP GUIDEBOOKS

Gardner (1975), in his chapter summarizing the research on the training of paraprofessionals, spoke of a "plethora of research and demonstration programs" and said that "the nonprofessional revolution in the mental health and mental retardation services delivery system has been nowhere more evident than in the area of behavior modification" (p. 469). As compared to more "traditional" psychotherapeutic approaches that rarely use paraprofessionals, behavior modification programs have been developed with parents, teachers, spouses, nurses, aides, and peers as some of the primary change agents. Paraprofessionals are used in data gathering as well as in the actual implementation of an intervention.

An excellent illustration of the use of paraprofessionals is the study by Adubato, Adams, and Budd (1981). They taught a parent (mother) to train her spouse in child management techniques for use with their brain-damaged son, who was severely developmentally delayed and had impaired motor coordination and hyperactivity. The experimenters taught the mother various techniques for improving her son's independent dressing skills. She was subsequently to teach these techniques to her husband, and they were both to apply them to the teaching of various new behaviors to their son. Results of this demonstration—including a two-year follow-up—indicated that the mother had successfully taught her husband the child management techniques she had been taught, that they both retained substantial portions of what they had learned, that they were still applying what they had learned, and that they were now able to control their son's behavior and add new skills to his repertoire above and beyond what had specifically been taught two years earlier. The efficiency, in terms of time and money, of the use of paraprofessionals is self-evident.

Further illustrating the widespread use of paraprofessionals, Rose (1980) describes "the organization, implementation, and evaluation of a behavioral in-service training program for paraprofessional staff in two group homes for mentally retarded adults" (p. 249). Tharp and Wetzel (1969) developed their behavioral intervention program, for implementation entirely in the natural environment, around the use of "Behavior Analysts (BA's)." These are "non-traditional, subprofessional" change agents, "selected specifically for their lack of previous training in any of the helping professions" (p. 62). In addition, Mash, Handy, and Hamerlynck (1976), in *Behavior Modification Approaches to Parenting,* have a five-chapter section dealing with various programs for training parents in systematic behavior management techniques. In their companion text, Mash, Hamerlynck, and Handy (1976) include a chapter dealing with the training of a child as the behavior change agent in family interactions.

Even Children as Therapists

Carden Smith and Fowler (1984) also used children as the "intervention agents" in their study. Children attending a remedial kindergarten program were taught how to administer points in a token economy system to their peers for a variety of appropriate, nondisruptive school behaviors (DRO). These points were later cashed in for the daily outdoor activity. Children who had earned at least three points could vote on which of several activities (e.g., kite, frisbee, softball) they wished to participate in. Two points allowed them to participate in the activity but not to vote. Fewer than two points meant that they had to remain indoors during the activity. The results showed that a peer-monitored (obviously nonprofessional) intervention could substantially reduce the children's disruptive behaviors. The authors demonstrated that "children, as young as kindergarten, can serve as mediators in a behavior management program and thus reduce the teacher's supervisory duties, at least partially. Furthermore, we demonstrate that even children with serious behavior and learning problems can effectively manage their peers' behavior and be managed by their peers" (p. 226).

Along with the advantages of using paraprofessionals, there are, obviously, certain *cautions.* Any time the therapist is removed from direct client contact, when someone else implements the intervention, a certain amount of confusion or inconsistency is possible. The therapist must be certain that the change agent understands the intervention, administers it as developed, and immediately reports any problems.

Self-Help Guides

With behavior modification applied in such a wide variety of settings and with such a broad population spectrum, coupled with the tremendous use of paraprofessionals, the natural outgrowth is the development of **self-help guides**. There seems to be a book describing the applicability of these procedures for nearly everyone. Books are specifically geared to parents of young children, parents of handicapped children, parents of teenagers, teenagers themselves, teachers, nurses, and business executives (e.g., from Research Press, Inc.). Some of the topics addressed are parenting, child management, skills training, teaching, assertiveness training, communication, obesity, cigarette smoking, and employee performance.

Watson and Tharp (1977) designed their book *Self-Directed Behavior: Self-Modification for Personal Adjustment* "to acquaint you with the general theory of behavior, to guide you through exercises for developing skills in self-analysis and to provide you with concrete information on how to achieve the goals you hold for yourself. . . . Any reader can use it for self-instruction; no 'prerequisites' are necessary. Clients of therapists or counselors can use it as an adjunct in planning their own self-change" (p. vii). Chapters provide the nonprofessional reader with instruction in such techniques as data recording, selecting reinforcers, the Premack principle, extinction, shaping, rehearsal, contracting, and self-punishment.

Schaefer and Millman (1981), acknowledging that "it's tough to be a parent" (p. v), wrote a text specifically for that population. Divided into six chapters, each devoted to a different broad classification, the book gives specific behavioral suggestions to help parents with 44 common behavior problems of children. The chapter titles include "Immature Behaviors," "Insecure Behaviors," "Habit Disorders," "Peer Problems," and "Antisocial Behaviors."

Azrin and Foxx (1974), having previously worked with a retarded population, developed a quick, home-based, parent-implemented toilet-training program for normal children. Their training procedure emphasizes "language ability, imagination, imitation, verbal rehearsal, and verbal instructions in addition to learning by association and learning by reward" (p. 10). The title of their book says it all: *Toilet Training in Less Than a Day.*

Clark (1986) reviews a videotape by Patterson and Forehand entitled *Time-Out!* In a series of vignettes with an 8- and 11-year-old, this tape instructs parents in the description, technique, practice, and precautions of time-out. Although not as accessible, perhaps, as a book, a videotape uses state-of-the-art technology to teach behavior modification techniques to a nonprofessional audience.

With the plethora of self-help guides available, a word of warning comes from Barlow (1980). He states that "the evidence supporting self-help books is either weak or nonexistent. . . . Until the data are in, it is possible that these self-help books are doing more harm than good" (p.

319). Barlow's argument revolves around the position that self-help treatment programs are rarely thoroughly and systematically evaluated. "Our careful, fine-grained analysis and technique-building approach" (p. 319), a historical underpinning of behavior modification, is applied to efficacy testing of self-help programs in only very superficial ways. In addition, because these guides are attuned to the "typical" problem, individual differences tend to be ignored. In these circumstances, a client may unknowingly implement an inappropriate intervention or overlook an important relevant variable—which could result in an inefficient or ineffective treatment program.

REFERRAL OR CONCURRENT TREATMENT

Referral to, or concurrent treatment by, a physician or other health-care professional should occur under several conditions. First, if the therapist and client cannot establish the appropriate therapeutic relationship (i.e., rapport), treatment effectiveness may suffer. Similarly, if the therapist lacks the appropriate knowledge, skills, or facilities, referral to another therapist is called for in the AABT ethical guidelines (see Table 6.1).

Referral to a physician should occur if the therapist believes there is some organic basis for the behavior or the use of medication seems warranted (as in severe depression or psychosis). It is good practice to have a client examined and assessed by a physician before implementing a behavioral intervention for such problems as enuresis, encopresis, seizures, obesity, sexual dysfunction, severe hyperkinesis, depression, and chronic pain disorders. Behavior modification can then be implemented along with possible medical treatment, or, at least, the medical information can be viewed as part of the client's "whole picture."

One potential problem, however, regarding the interaction between behavior therapists (usually doctors of psychology) and physicians, including psychiatrists, is the minimal influence on the medical community and its low appreciation of behavior modification, operant conditioning, and contingency management. Moss and Rick (1981b), in a comprehensive review of the literature on adolescent psychiatry, conclude, "Clearly, psychiatry as a profession has not embraced operant technology in the treatment of adolescent disorders. Speculation can be raised whether psychiatrists adhere to more traditional approaches because they are not exposed to operant technology either through training or through continuing medical education. Certainly, only an occasional report can be found in the psychiatric literature, in contrast to the literature in other, nonmedical disciplines" (p. 1166).

Like Moss and Rick, I also reviewed two volumes (vol. 141, 1984, and vol. 142, 1985) of *The American Journal of Psychiatry,* the "official journal of the American Psychiatric Association." Looking through the table of contents at the titles of all the published articles, I noticed that only 4 of the more than 500 regular articles, special articles, brief communications, and clinical and research reports appeared to involve any behavioral intervention. The behavior therapist, therefore, may have to "educate" physicians in the applicability and efficacy of behavior modification in what they may view as either a strictly medical problem or as a psychological problem requiring a "traditional" interpretation and approach.

With the increase of behavioral deficits and the decrease of behavioral excesses as the goals of behavior modification, any classification system that allows behavior problems to be viewed along this continuum is applicable. The American Psychiatric Association's *DSM*–III-R (1987), although not using this nomenclature, does categorize most of the behavior problems discussed in this text.

Disorder	Code Number
attention deficit disorders:	
with hyperactivity	314.01
conduct disorders:	
aggression	312.00
elective mutism	313.23
oppositional disorder	313.81
violation of rules	
temper tantrums	
eating disorders:	
anorexia nervosa	307.10
alcohol intoxication	303.00
psychogenic pain	307.80
academic problems	V62.30
noncompliance with medical treatment	V15.81
parent-child problem	V61.20
compulsive disorder	300.30
passive-aggressive disorder	301.84
gambling	312.31
stuttering	307.00
enuresis	307.60
encopresis	307.70
explosive disorder	312.34
impulse-control disorder	312.39

CRITERIA FOR TERMINATION

"Behavior therapy does not conceptualize maladaptive responding as emanating from a 'disturbed personality.' Obviously, then, the goal of the therapist and client would not be to facilitate the reorganizing or restructuring of the client's personality. Instead, the aim would be to help to alleviate the specific problems that are interfering with the client's functioning" (Rimm & Masters, 1979, p. 8). With this as the treatment goal, the criteria for termination should be relatively clear and straightforward.

If the therapist and client have engaged in the collaborative effort of operationally defining the target behavior; placing it along the deficit-excess continuum; and explicitly measuring it within its quantifiable characteristics of frequency, duration, and intensity, the point at which therapy can terminate has, in fact, been predetermined. If appropriate pre- and postintervention data are available, improvement or lack of improvement can be compared to this objective criterion.

Chapter
7

Special Problems
to Consider

Walker and Shea (1980) make the grandiose claim that "it should be stressed here that behavior modification always works. The failure of an intervention does not lie in the principles of behavior modification but in the application of those principles by the practitioner" (p. 40). Although everyone might not agree with the quantitative nature of that statement, it is clearly the case that many interventions either don't succeed or have limited success because of methodological problems. Unfortunately, most of these "failures" do not find their way into the literature and, thus, cannot help others avoid the same pitfalls.

One such study, however, is that by Patterson and Jackson (1980). Working with six geriatric residents, aged 61 to 79, they implemented a contingency management program to help treat incontinence. Although their behavioral intervention involved a "pants check" every two hours and cigarettes and conversation with staff when dry (tangible and social reinforcers, respectively), no significant improvement was observed. Two of the possible reasons for failure include the relatively low frequency of reinforcement (maximum once every two hours); also, because of such problems as severe memory deficits, some of the patients showed an inability to locate the bathroom. A problem-solving approach, as illustrated by Patterson and Jackson, should be a part of any contingency management program. The following are several of the more common problems faced in the implementation of a behavior modification program.

COMPLIANCE

Because of the emphasis behavior modification places on the collaborative effort of the therapist and client, and because of its reliance on the active participation of the client in the implementation of a treatment plan, compliance with a contingency management program is essential. Noncompliance, then, can be a serious problem. This is more frequently the case with clients who have not voluntarily sought help and who may not even acknowledge that a problem exists. Although it is possible with the use of contingency management to bring a nonmotivated client to therapy and even to get that person to perform certain limited behaviors, the efficiency of such an intervention is certainly questionable. (See also the section on Adherence to Treatment Regimens in Chapter 5.)

Fortunately, most therapists see clients with at least some stated commitment to change. When compliance regarding various assessment and implementation tasks remains a problem, one must examine its possible causes. These tend to fall into three categories.

First, when a client doesn't engage in a reinforced behavior, it could be due to either **low reinforcer value** or a problem with reinforcer administration. Since a reinforcer is defined by its effectiveness, if a behavior is not maintained by its consequences, those consequences might not be reinforcers or potent enough reinforcers for that client at that time. Noncompliance because of these reasons can be reduced through the use of reinforcer survey schedules, client-selected reinforcers, frequently changed reinforcers to prevent satiation, and an adjustment or analysis of deprivation conditions. For example, I developed a token economy for a child with the reinforcer of going swimming on Saturday afternoon. After several weeks, when it became apparent that the desired behavior was not being emitted with sufficient frequency for the Saturday swims, I discovered that the parents were noncontingently taking the child swimming on Tuesdays and Thursdays. An adjustment of the deprivation state, and hence the perceived value of the reinforcer, led to an increase in compliance.

Occasionally, the reinforcer itself is of sufficient value, but there is a problem with **reinforcer administration**. For example, the person responsible for reinforcing the appropriate behavior either might fail to do so or might impose a lengthy delay of reinforcement. In these conditions—response emitted without reinforcement—extinction might take place and the intervention won't work.

Frequently, the person responsible for the administration of the positive reinforcer feels that it is wrong, or should not be necessary, to reinforce a behavior that "should" be made anyway. This is a commonly held position by many parents seeking help with a noncompliant child—one who does not do assigned chores or obey parental demands. The parents more frequently notice and comment on undesirable behaviors while ignoring (extinguishing) desired behaviors because they "are expected." A similar problem with reinforcer administration involves the conversion of positive reinforcement very obviously into punishment, for example, by the parent who might say, "Here's the money I owe you because of that damn contract!"

In these circumstances, the therapist must elicit the understanding and cooperation of the change agent. That the desired behavior is not currently being emitted with sufficient frequency, that the proposed program does work, that what has previously been tried hasn't worked, and that we all receive and enjoy reinforcements (e.g., salary for work) are some of the arguments used to enlist the necessary support.

Fairchild (1985) describes the development of a joint home and school token economy program. The school officials and the parents were actively involved in the planning, development, and implementation of the treatment plan. "Long-term gains," it is noted, "typically require that significant others . . . support and assist in the intervention process" (p. 141). Moreover, "implementation of a token economy system requires communication with the parents and willingness of parents and teachers to share the responsibility for helping the child to develop appropriate behaviors" (p. 142). Without this cooperation, the program would either have to be drastically modified or, quite simply, just wouldn't work.

Reinforcer administration is even a problem when the persons responsible are the clients themselves. Some people feel "foolish" or "childish" for rewarding themselves or believe that it runs counter to some long-held tenet that one must not be boastful. Again, the existence of the current behavior problem and the efficacy of the procedure are the key arguments for its use.

Second, when a task is not performed, it is sometimes *too difficult* or *too large a step* from the preceding response; that is, it was improperly shaped. A child might not comply with the task of completely making the bed or getting dressed, but he or she might comply with the response of straightening the blanket or pulling on a pair of pants. Similarly, an agoraphobic client might not drive to the nearest shopping center if the immediately preceding response in the shaping hierarchy was merely pulling the car in and out of the driveway at home.

Third, compliance problems could reflect the fact that the desired response, if emitted, might be not only positively reinforced but simultaneously *negatively punished* as well. In other words, the reinforced desired response could concurrently lead to the termination or elimination of some other pleasant consequences. For example, think of the schoolchild who receives private tutoring sessions contingent on doing poorly in math. If grades were to go up, this individual attention might be lost. If tutoring can thus be viewed by this child as a positive reinforcer, doing poorly in math could be viewed as an operant, maintained by its consequences. A parental contingency management program aimed at improving math grades will put the child into an obvious approach-avoidance conflict and contribute to compliance problems. In such circumstances, one attempts to reduce the conflict by making the positive reinforcers for the emission of the desired response quantitatively or qualitatively greater than the positive reinforcer that might be lost.

RELAPSE PREVENTION

Contingency management is caught up in the proverbial "catch-22"—if you win, you lose. As Kanfer and Phillips (1970) put it, "the ABAB design, necessary to demonstrate the relevance of the clinical intervention to a behavior change, by its very nature denies the durability of the effects. If the reversal phase increases again the problem response and thus confirms that the therapist has established the desired control over the patient's behavior, it also demonstrates that the newly strengthened behavior decreases as soon as the therapist's systematic reinforcement is withdrawn" (p. 276). Thus, the most commonly observed procedure for demonstrating the (short-term) effectiveness of contingency management simultaneously demonstrates its ineffectiveness to prevent (long-term) relapse after the intervention is terminated. The previously discussed Dapcich-Miura and Hovell (1979) study (Figure 4.2) clearly shows that during the return to baseline phase (second B), the behaviors revert to their original frequency.

Similarly, Roberts and Fanurik (1986), who increased the use of seat belts from 4.3 percent to 66.2 percent with a group contingency management procedure, found a reduction in compliance to 17.2 percent and 8.5 percent during the 14-week and 18-week nonrewarded follow-up observations. Again, McCaul, Stitzer, Bigelow, and Liebson (1984), who produced an increase in opiate-free urine tests in a group of methadone maintenance patients with a contingency management program, report that "during subsequent weeks the percentage of clean urines decreased gradually" (p. 38) and that "the contingency management program . . . [merely] slowed the rate of relapse" (p. 41).

Although these results are discouraging, they should not be surprising. Contrary to the medical model of illness, which talks of a cure, contingency management views behavior "as a function of the environment, and when the environment is altered, behavior can be altered" (Bellack & Hersen, 1977, p. 22). In fact, because behavior is so often a function of its consequences, one should be *more* surprised if when contingencies were reversed, behavior did *not* reverse! From a practical point of view, however, the important question revolves around *maintaining behavior change.*

Maintenance

The procedure that has perhaps received the most attention regarding relapse and relapse prevention, and the one that epitomizes contingency management, is the token economy. Although there is little question of the ability of a token economy to produce behavior change while the contingencies are in effect, a number of variables make the transition from a token system to the natural environment difficult and, hence, limit the maintenance of the behavior. Any system that regularly, immediately, and tangibly reinforces common daily behaviors will engender relapse when the contingency is terminated. It is a simple fact of life, for example, that many of the behaviors maintained on an in-patient token economy ward are rarely reinforced in the same ways in the natural environment. These include many personal hygiene and social behaviors and, therefore, explain the extinction and subsequent recidivism frequently observed once the patient is discharged.

Reducing the Incongruence

The key to relapse prevention is the reduction in the incongruence between the contingency management system and the natural environment. "This potential problem with the use of token systems is a specific case of the more general need for any artificial treatment environment to manage the transfer and maintenance of new behaviors in the patient's natural daily environment. . . . When an artificial treatment setting can gradually incorporate more and more segments of the larger, more natural environment, and fade out the prosthetic devices . . . patients are gradually forced to deal more with the persons and events they will later encounter in society outside of the artificial community in which treatment occurs" (Kanfer & Phillips, 1970, p. 308). Reducing this incongruence can be accomplished in several ways, including changes in the frequency, magnitude, form, and locus of reinforcement (Bandura, 1969; Kazdin, 1978).

Once behavior change has been established, contingent reinforcement should be gradually "thinned out" to a more variable ratio or interval schedule so that the desired behavior is made more frequently or for longer periods of time without reinforcement. These schedules have been demonstrated to produce considerably more resistance to extinction than does continuous reinforcement. Katz and Vinciguerra (1982) systematically investigated "the effects of informational variables that accompany the transition from a high to low density schedule of reinforcement" (p. 21). The authors varied the explanation for the thinning of reinforcement three ways and found that (1) "a personal competence set" ("You're doing such a good job today I don't think you need as many tokens") maintained behavior to an average of 87 percent as compared to prethinning baselevel; (2) "a no-information condition" maintained behavior to an average of 78 percent; and (3) "an external attribution set" (thinning was attributed to "factors beyond the child's control such as shortened supplies of tokens") maintained behavior to an average of only 54 percent (p. 21). The authors concluded that "it has become almost axiomatic to prescribe intermittent reinforcement when durable behavior change is desired.

However, results of this study suggest that more than reinforcement variables need to be considered. The information that accompanies schedule changes . . . also exerts functional control over behavior" (p. 22).

In addition to changes in the schedule of reinforcement, the amount of reinforcement can be gradually reduced and the type of reinforcement can be changed. It has been previously suggested that social reinforcers should be administered concurrently with any tangible rewards: "Joe, you paid attention and didn't miss a word. Good work! Here's a sticker" (Brown, Fagua, & Otts, 1986, p. 601). This is especially important because the natural environment places increasing value on this type of reinforcer. If, through sufficient pairings, the verbalizations become conditioned reinforcers, they can maintain behavior in the absence of tangible or primary rewards.

Perhaps most important, as the behavior of the client improves, the locus of reinforcement shifts from the change agent to peer group members and to the client himself or herself. This shift is from external, extrinsic reinforcement to internal, intrinsic reinforcement, with the client delivering the consequences. For example, to a child whose aggressive outbursts are reduced to the point where he or she can now derive substantial enjoyment from play and other interactions with children, this enjoyment takes over as both the motivation and reinforcement for the reduction of aggression. In these conditions, withdrawal of formal, change-agent reinforcement can be more easily accomplished. Rimm and Masters (1979), among others, use the term *behavior trap* to summarize this important phenomenon—that "the initial behavior manipulation (by contingency management) of a few client behaviors may provide an entry to an environment that provides naturalistic reinforcement contingencies that maintain those behaviors and shape new ones" (p. 266). Tharp and Wetzel (1969) developed a variety of procedures and strategies for the implementation of behavior modification programs entirely in the natural environment.

Kazdin (1977), in his book *The Token Economy,* reiterates the position that "the contingencies need not be continued indefinitely to maintain behavior and need not be extended to each situation in which transfer is desired. Various techniques are available that are likely to postpone or eliminate the loss of behavioral gains made during a reinforcement program and to ensure that changes transfer to situations in which the contingencies have not been in effect" (p. 178). As review, he outlines eight strategies, including selecting behaviors that are likely to be maintained by the natural environment, fading the contingencies, scheduling intermittent reinforcement, delaying reinforcer delivery, and self-reinforcement (pp. 178–193).

Marlatt's "Relapse Prevention Model"

In 1985, there was an intensive series of professional meetings referred to as the National Working Conference on Smoking Relapse, sponsored by the National Heart, Lung, and Blood Institute. Two of the conference leaders stressed the importance of the meeting by stating, "We know how to help people quit smoking, and we are rather successful at it; we know little about how to prevent relapse, and we fail miserably" (Shumaker & Grunberg, 1986, p. 69). Therefore, one of the task forces at this conference specifically reviewed various interventions aimed at preventing relapse. Some of the strategies discussed were better preparation for quitting, including the development of more realistic attitudes and expectations; increasing commitment to quitting, including the use of incentives to increase motivation; development of more effective social support systems and self-reward strategies; development of various coping skills, including relaxation training; and general life-style changes to find and develop new reinforcers and reinforced behaviors to help compensate for the loss of smoking. The task force participants noted the "working" nature of the conference and that much more research needed to be done before the relapse problem could be solved.

One of the presenters at this conference was G. Alan Marlatt, who coauthored a paper entitled "Understanding and Preventing Relapse: Commonalities Across Addictive Disorders." Working predominantly in the field of alcohol addiction, Marlatt has developed what he calls the **Relapse Prevention (RP) Model**. Marlatt and George (1984) describe this self-control program, noting that "In contrast with traditional approaches that overemphasize initial habit change, RP focuses more on the maintenance phase of the habit change process. . . . RP treatment procedures include specific intervention techniques designed to teach the individual to effectively anticipate and cope with potential relapse situations" (p. 261). Specifically, therefore, RP is a behavioral maintenance program.

As a basic premise of the Relapse Prevention Model, clients are taught how to recognize high-risk situations, that is, those likely to be associated with the possibility of relapse. They are then trained in various problem-solving techniques and taught to generate alternative behaviors or coping skills. Many of the procedures used to teach these skills are those behavioral methods previously discussed in this text. According to Chaney, O'Leary, and Marlatt (1978), they include "instruction, modeling, behavioral rehearsal, and coaching" (p. 1096). Eventually, the authors report, clients "were taught how to define the problems that a situation presented . . . and to generate alternatives and think about the long- and short-term consequences" (p. 1096). According to Marlatt, there is growing empirical support for RP.

Follow-up

The systematic examination of relapse and relapse prevention has been consistently and seriously hampered by a scarcity of follow-up data reported in the literature. Agras and Berkowitz (1980) reviewed the 1970–1978 volumes of *Behavior Therapy* and *Behaviour Research and Therapy* and found the median duration of follow-up to be only four weeks. LaDouceur and Auger (1980) looked for the presence or absence of six-month follow-up data. Reviewing the literature, they state that previous investigators found that only 8.8 percent and 12 percent of studies inventoried included a follow-up of such duration. In their study, they examined seven behavior therapy journals from the first year of publication until 1978. Approximately 25 percent of all the studies reviewed included six-month or more follow-up data. This percentage, however, varied greatly depending on the specific journal reviewed. Whereas the *Journal of Behavior Therapy and Experimental Psychiatry* showed an average of better than 50 percent, *Behavior Therapy* averaged 25 percent, and the *Journal of Applied Behavior Analysis* showed an average of less than 10 percent.

Although the use of *booster sessions* as an additional method of relapse prevention makes sense, there seems to be little systematic investigation or utilization of this technique in the behavior modification literature. This may, in part, be a reflection of the overall scarcity of follow-up as previously discussed. Clearly, however, if a client returns to a therapist because the behavior problem has returned, the evaluation, analysis, and course of therapy to follow could be considered to be in the form of a booster, albeit not prophylactic.

Rose (1977) recommends a 3-, 6-, or 12-month follow-up interview or session after the termination of a group. These sessions can be used to assess maintenance or act as a "booster shot" for maintaining behavior changes. A specific homework assignment given at the final meeting could act as preparation for this follow-up group session. However, Rose acknowledges the difficulty in getting group members to return and suggests that, perhaps, long-range follow-up might have to occur by telephone. He believes that periodic contact between the therapist and client (initiated by either party) can be effective as a maintenance technique.

PRECAUTIONS AND CONTRAINDICATIONS OF IMPLEMENTATION

Many of the behavior modification procedures previously described in this text have, or should have, associated precautions. Some of these have already been discussed. Without these precautions, a successful intervention is less likely. Following are seven major precautions:

1. If the *target behavior is not explicitly defined* (i.e., all the parties involved do not have a clear understanding of what behavior is or is not to be performed), confusion and inefficiency result. For example, consider a teacher who develops a contract with the children in his or her class. If they are "good" during the morning, afternoon recess will be extended. This is a typical situation in that the target behavior (being "good") is far too vague. What results is a day-to-day inconsistency between what the children do and what follows. At best, this intervention will be only marginally successful.

2. If one is not aware that *reinforcers are not intuitive*, the temptation is to use what works with one client blindly with another. Thus, it is possible that occasionally, because of individual client differences, what is intended to be a positive reinforcer will turn out to be a negative reinforcer or vice versa. Clearly the results of such an intervention will be radically different from what is expected or desired.

3. If one either shapes too quickly or has too few intermediary responses between the ultimately desired response and the behavior already in the client's repertoire, *extinction* could take place. Extinction also occurs when one goes too quickly from continuous reinforcement to a very partial intermittent schedule. In either case, extinction results when the client makes too many nonreinforced responses.

4. One should always use a *DRO technique* simultaneously with any of the other techniques described to reduce a behavioral excess. The use of DRO is necessitated by the fact that these other procedures fail to teach appropriate and desired behavior. With a suppression or reduction of the excess, a "behavioral vacuum" is formed that may be filled with another undesired behavior. If a child has a temper tantrum because of the resulting parental attention it engenders, extinguishing this response alone could result in the development of another inappropriate behavior (e.g., breaking windows) for the reinforcement (attention) that follows. DRO, however, teaches an appropriate means of attaining reinforcing attention while the tantrum is reduced. This approach is clearly more pleasant and effective.

5. If one uses *extinction,* it should be understood that the graphic representation (curve) of a response undergoing extinction is usually a very irregular one. Response rate often rises at first, and the behavior becomes more variable and intense (see Figure 4.3). Only gradually does the response rate decrease; moreover, extinction rarely shows a smooth response decrease. Two problems result from this initial rise in rate and intensity, especially if they are not anticipated. First, thinking the technique is not working, the change agent may abandon it long before success would have been obtained. Second, the quantitative and qualitative increases in the behavior (e.g., tantrums) are frequently difficult to tolerate. Occasionally, the change agent (parent) "gives in." This type of intermittent reinforcement makes subsequent extinction all the more difficult.

6. While using the various procedures aimed at reducing behavioral excesses, one must be cautious not to reinforce the very behavior one is trying to eliminate. Time-out, for example, is supposed to be the removal of the client to a presumably nonreinforcing environment. Occasionally, however, if a student is sent into the hall, he or she is chosen as a courier, carrying messages around the school building. Many children find this type of job highly reinforcing, and, therefore, the behavior that led to this opportunity (Premack principle) is not reduced in frequency.

7. A number of precautions concern the implementation of a *punishment procedure.* Aside from the fact that punishment merely suppresses behavior and, like extinction and time-out, fails to provide an acceptable

alternative behavior, it raises a host of ethical and legal questions (to be discussed later in this chapter). In addition, as an iatrogenic effect, it often generates various emotional reactions, such as anxiety, fear, and anger, toward the environment and people involved in its implementation. And perhaps most important, positive punishment can be abused, resulting in physical harm to the client. For example, Ruprecht, Hanson, Pocrnich, and Murphy (1980) warn against the use of lemon juice (citric acid) as a punisher. Some of the possible medical complications include an irritation of the interior and exterior of the mouth, the possibility of aspiration or gagging and its subsequent irritation of the lungs, and the erosion and decalcification of tooth enamel.

Contraindication is defined as a *circumstance indicating the inappropriateness of a treatment.* Behavior modification procedures may be contraindicated in certain conditions.

Punishment and other aversive procedures are contraindicated unless three conditions are met. First, more intrusive and aversive procedures are inappropriate unless all less intrusive and less aversive procedures have been tried and shown to be not effective. Second, aversive procedures are contraindicated unless accompanied by DRO. And third, aversive procedures are contraindicated unless the legal status of the client is considered, the procedure is reviewed, and informed consent is obtained.

Even positive reinforcement procedures can be contraindicated in certain circumstances. When an analysis of the client's prior learning history and the conditions of the current maladaptive behavior indicate that it might not be an operant, a modification of contingencies could prove to be an inappropriate intervention strategy. In addition, if there is a problem with reinforcer administration, interventions involving these procedures might again be contraindicated. The appropriateness of any given contingency management procedure necessarily depends on the completeness and accuracy of the assessment, the therapist's ability to implement the intervention, the particular therapeutic setting (home, school, institution, etc.), the age of the client, and the availability of any required equipment. The therapist's job is to form a "best fit" among the client, setting, maladaptive behavior, and treatment.

The procedures described in this text can be effectively and safely used if these precautions are observed and contraindications considered.

ETHICAL AND LEGAL ISSUES

Ethics

The major ethical issue surrounding behavior modification and, more specifically, contingency management involves the notion of *control.* The technological advances of the past few decades have, in fact, increased one's ability to change (i.e., control) another person's behavior; thus, the specter of totalitarianism has been raised. The questions being asked include the following: Who are the controllers? Who gives them the right to control? How will they control? Who will be controlled and why?

These same questions could just as reasonably (and, perhaps, should) be asked concerning "traditional" psychotherapy, medicine, biological research, law and government, and education. It should be stressed that the use of surgical procedures, electrode implantation, drugs, recombinant DNA, cloning, sensory deprivation, incarceration, capital punishment, and electronic surveillance are *not* a part of behavior modification.

The procedures of contingency management described in this text all have a common and central theme. They involve a reversible alteration of the contingent relationship in order to change a behavior in a clearly defined manner as determined collaboratively by the therapist and client. In a definitional statement emphasizing this point, Bellack and Hersen (1977) speak of behavior modification as an "applied discipline with the goal of alleviating human distress and modifying behavior for the benefit of the individual and society. The emphasis of intervention is on education rather than manipulation. Rather than exerting control over the client, behavior modification expects him to be an active participant in treatment, helping to select goals, plan treatment techniques, and learn to control his own behavior and environment" (pp. 21–22).

Client's rights, vis-à-vis contingency management, are safeguarded in several ways. The ethical standards adopted and provided by AABT (1977) call for full disclosure and collaboration between the therapist and client or agent of the client (see Table 6.1). The agreement that positive reinforcement procedures are always used before aversives, that DRO is always employed concurrently with aversives, and that positive punishment procedures are always "last-resort" procedures sets up an important methodological schema. This intervention hierarchy, or continuum of intrusiveness, helps ensure that minimum effective force will be employed and that needless discomfort or unpleasantness will be avoided. The use of "human rights committees" (Risley & Sheldon-Wildgen, 1980) further protects the client by ensuring that potentially controversial treatment programs are thoroughly reviewed before their implementation. I have been a member of a state Department of Education Commission charged with the development of a set of guidelines for the use of behavior management techniques in special education classrooms; a member of the Human Rights and Behavior Management Committee of a large, private special education facility; and a member of a state Department of Mental Retardation Program Review Committee. In all cases, the safety and rights of the client remained of paramount importance as various behavior modification interventions were developed, reviewed, and implemented.

Legality

Although not necessarily directed specifically at behavior modification, a number of court cases in recent years have affected the applicability and utilization of certain contingency management procedures. Primarily involving institutionalized individuals, the legal issue revolves around the potential conflict between the aims and methods of changing behavior on the one hand and the individual's civil rights on the other. The major question concerns treatment curtailing rights normally granted, including due process and equal protection. White and White (1981) review several recent federal district court cases that "decided that institutionalized patients have a qualified constitutional right to refuse psychotropic medications. . . . These cases differentiate the right of the state to remove persons from the community because of psychological disturbances that create dangers of harm from the issue of whether the state can impose treatment" on such persons (p. 954). These cases, however, speak only of the right to refuse psychotropic medication, not necessarily other psychotherapeutic interventions. Martin (1975) and Kazdin (1978) provide extensive reviews of the legal challenges.

As related to contingency management, the legal issues and court decisions fall into several categories. In terms of the selection of target behaviors—for example, what behaviors earn token reinforcement—the court has ruled "that if the only purpose of patient work [was] saving money and effort for the institution, and not therapeutic value, the individual's constitutional rights may [have been] violated. . . . Patients could be assigned some work if the tasks were reasonably related to a therapeutic program" (Kazdin, 1978, p. 354). The court did not, however, clearly define "therapeutic program."

Many of the court's decisions leave room for interpretation. For example, the use of aversive techniques—including electric shock for retarded clients—has been allowed, but only under "extraordinary circumstances such as self-destructive behavior that was likely to inflict physical damage" (Kazdin, 1978, p. 352). However, to further protect the rights of the individual, the court continued, "Shock could only be applied after other procedures had been attempted, after approval from a committee on human rights, and with informed consent from the client or a relative, and under direct order of the institution's superintendent" (p. 353). The client's (i.e., prisoner's) right to refuse aversive treatment may be "sacrificed when the state wishes to protect against some grave and immediate danger" (p. 357).

Perhaps the legal decision with the greatest impact for contingency management involves the distinction between "rights" and "privileges." A landmark court case* mandated that institutionalized populations are entitled to certain amenities frequently used as privileges, for example, in token economy systems. Previously used as backup reinforcers, these "rights" must now be available on a noncontingent basis: "access to a room, bed, meals, clothes, improvements in each of these over very mini-

---

*Wyatt v. Stickney, 344 F. Supp. 373, 344 F. Supp. 387 (M.D. Ala. 1972).

mal facilities, recreational activities, home visits, access to private space, and attending religious services" (Kazdin, 1978, p. 347).

Although these rights present obvious problems for operant-based programs, the legal issue *must* take precedence. However, several alternative solutions do exist. Clients may, for example, voluntarily waive certain rights—thus providing for effective reinforcers—as part of treatment. In addition, new reinforcers, beyond the "basic amenities," are being sought and used. In conclusion, Matson (1980) states that "the contingent use of primary comforts as reinforcers for prosocial behaviors resulted in a social outcry of violations of certain legal rights. . . . It has been thought advisable not to deprive patients of items they are accustomed to having without charge. Rather, reinforcers that are not ordinarily available should be added to the hospital environment" as the rewards of contingency management interventions (p. 171).

To summarize, behavior modification has traditionally sought to *alleviate* human suffering. Whatever changes are necessitated by the preceding ethical and legal issues must be made so that this goal can be achieved.

Chapter
8

The Years to Come

This text has repeatedly stressed that behavior modification is empirical, that is, research- and data-based. As "experimental-clinical psychology," behavior modification is tied to the published literature and is, therefore, constantly growing and evolving as a discipline. Having taught you the techniques or procedures of current behavioral practice, I now leave you with some thoughts about its future direction.

COGNITIVE BEHAVIOR MODIFICATION

As described in Chapter 1, one of the basic historical tenets of behaviorism is the repudiation of consciousness as psychology's primary domain of study. Watson, as you will recall, argued that one need be concerned only with objective, measurable, observable, overt behavior. Within approximately the past ten years, however, a departure from this strict or "radical" behavioral position has occurred. First referred to as "the cognitive-learning perspective," it is the realization that "thoughts, feelings, and behaviors are causally interactive" (Mahoney, 1977, p. 8). In other words, it is the understanding that much of what one does (overt or public behavior) is a reflection of what one thinks or, if you will, says to oneself (covert, or inner or private, behavior). The ultimate aim of what has evolved into **cognitive behavior modification** is still, of course, overt behavior change, but the techniques and procedures first involve changing inner behavior.

Mahoney (1977) acknowledges that this development may seem to be quite a departure from traditional behavior modification. He notes, however, that "despite their long history of often bitter rivalry, behaviorists and cognitive psychologists appear to be cautiously easing into the same theoretical bed" (p. 5). What has allowed this synthesis of what could be viewed as opposing forces to be accepted by the general behavioral community is the fact that cognitive behavior therapists are still behavior therapists, that is, still behaviorally oriented. Their goal is not merely cognitive alteration (as might be the case with more "traditional" psychotherapy) but also clear, overt behavior change. Moreover, there is the firm conviction that cognitions (thoughts) are, in fact, behaviors and, as such, "are subject to the same laws of learning as are overt behaviors" (Kendall & Hollon, 1979, p. 5).

According to such cognitive behavior therapists as Kendall and Hollon (1979), such inner behaviors or cognitions as attitudes, beliefs, thoughts, perceptions, attributions, and expectancies "are central to producing, predicting, and understanding psychopathological behavior" (p. 5). That is, if one's behavior is affected by one's cognitions (what one thinks influences what one does), "appropriate" cognitions can produce adaptive behaviors, and "inappropriate" or "faulty" cognitions can produce maladaptive or problematic behaviors. Martin and Pear (1983) explain this concept by noting that "a major theoretical assumption of cognitive therapy is that individuals interpret and react to events in terms of their perceived significance, that is, that human behavior is mediated by cognition. A second theoretical assumption is that cognitive deficiencies can cause emotional disorders" (p. 422).

For example, I treated a client suffering from depression, and many of his cognitions fit the following pattern: One day at work he was transferred from one project to another within his department. He interpreted this switch in job assignment as a personal affront: "I must have been incompetent on that job and they had to take it away from me." These cognitions or beliefs led to feelings of self-depreciation and depression ("I'm no good") and, subsequently, to a number of corresponding problematic behaviors (crying, arguments at home, lethargy, loss of appetite, decreased sexual interest). As one can see, the way he thought—what he said to himself—ultimately affected his overt behaviors. The analysis of this client's problem is certainly consistent with the cognitive theory of depression outlined by Hollon and Beck (1979). They conclude that "depression is, in part, a consequence of pervasive, negative misconstructions of objective experience" (p. 154).

It is important to note that there are alternative (i.e., more adaptive) ways for this client to have interpreted the original event. Couldn't he have been transferred to another project because of some special skill or ability he possessed? In fact, at my suggestion, he asked his supervisor. Yes, they *needed him* on the second job. Anyone at all in the office could complete the original assignment. If this second explanation of the event had been part of his primary belief system, perhaps some of the ultimate depression could have been avoided. This, then, is the aim and scope of cognitive behavior modification: "The primary focus of therapy is a fundamental change in a client's cognitions. Thus . . . cognitive behavior modifiers speak of achieving desirable changes in a client's behavior . . . by altering thought patterns, beliefs, attitudes, and opinions" (Martin & Pear, 1983, p. 422). In other words, one needs to modify private behavior to bring about a change in public behavior.

Ellis and Beck

Two of the pioneers in the field of cognitive behavior modification are Albert Ellis and Aaron Beck. Ellis developed a model of therapy referred to as **Rational-Emotive Therapy (RET)**. (See, for example, Ellis & Harper, 1975.) It posits the relationship between what one says and thinks and how one feels. Moreover, it postulates that various psychological disorders derive from irrational patterns of thinking that are either explicit or implicit self-verbalizations ("internal dialogue"). Therapy, therefore, involves the restructuring of these cognitions. Clients are taught—perhaps with modeling and behavioral rehearsal—to counteract such irrational self-statements with more positive and realistic statements. According to Bellack and Hersen (1977), "clients are trained to think differently, to evaluate the environment differently, to problem solve, and to think rationally" (p. 127).

Beck, too, revolves his cognitive therapy around the alteration of dysfunctional or distorted thoughts. (See, for example, Beck & Emery, 1985.) These maladaptive self-verbalizations ("automatic thoughts") fall into three common categories (the "cognitive triad"): negative interpretations of events, dislike of self, and negative appraisal of the future. Clients must learn to counteract these negative self-statements. According to Hollon and Beck (1979), the "cognitive-behavioral approach to treatment [is] designed to identify, evaluate, and change these maladaptive belief systems and dysfunctional styles of information processing" (p. 154).

For example, I treated a client who suffered from anxiety in a variety of social settings. One day—after therapy had been progressing for a while—she attended a football game. This was not an easy situation for her, and she felt somewhat apprehensive. At one point during the game she leapt to her feet to cheer a touchdown. Suddenly she felt lightheaded and dizzy. Although she began to tell herself that this was the beginning of a major anxiety attack and that she would have to leave the stadium and go home (the maladaptive thoughts), she remembered what she had been taught and caught herself. She quickly substituted—as a clearly more adaptive thought—the idea that the physical feelings she was experiencing were the result of the sudden postural change she had made and the resulting low blood pressure. She then began to notice that the physical sensations were dissipating and she was able to stay and enjoy the remainder of the game.

Reynolds and Coats (1986) developed a more systematic example—a ten-session cognitive behavioral training program for the treatment of depression in adolescents. Various sessions focused on teaching self-monitoring and self-observation; understanding the relationship among self-statements, feelings, and behavior; analyzing a number of common distortions or errors of thinking; and developing realistic and obtainable self-change plans. In sum, the subjects were "encouraged to continue using cognitive-behavioral procedures . . . that emphasized the training of self-control skills, including self-monitoring, self-evaluation, and self-reinforcement" beyond the formal training program, into the future (p. 655).

As one looks into the future, the scope and role of cognitive behavior modification will certainly grow. What one should expect, however, is that the specific techniques or procedures will become more formalized or concretized in much the same way as are the other behavioral procedures described in this text. Presently, they are perhaps too vaguely described to be used effectively by such groups as paraprofessionals, parents, and students. In this regard, they currently differ from the older, more "established" behavior modification procedures.

VARIOUS LOOSE ENDS

As one reads this text, a number of methodological problems, unanswered questions, and areas for future research certainly arise. The answers obtained will surely alter and form the practice of behavior modification over the course of your professional careers. The following is a sample of these "loose ends."

First, based on the literature reviewed, it appears that *maintenance,* or *relapse prevention,* is a topic that has not yet received adequate attention. Intimately related to relapse is the practice of long-term follow-up. As was indicated, very few studies follow clients beyond the actual active intervention period, and those that do frequently follow for only a short period of time. The efficacy of the field depends on more than a short-lived behavior change; it should depend on relatively permanent improvement. How can one speak of the success of a clinical intervention when the client is rarely observed for as long as even several months following treatment? As the practice of longer-term follow-ups increases (as is urged by LaDouceur & Auger, 1980), various techniques to prevent relapse that are not currently used—such as booster sessions—will need to be developed, researched, delineated, and validated.

Second, the area of client *compliance* seems to be one needing further exploration. Most therapists have had their share of clients classified as "non-doers." After a period of "non-doing," most of these people drop out of therapy, not having shown any significant improvement. What are the factors or conditions surrounding this problem, and how can it be better controlled?

Third, do reinforcement systems, the essential key components of contingency management, have any, perhaps subtle, adverse side effects?

In their article "Token Rewards May Lead to Token Learning," Levine and Fasnacht (1974) warn that "by automatically giving tokens for tasks, although the task will be completed, there is the risk that the intrinsic satisfaction of the task will be decreased" (p. 820). They present the results of a number of studies (e.g., Deci, 1971) that indicate that "extrinsic" reinforcement diminishes whatever "intrinsic" reinforcement a task may hold. Therefore, when therapist-controlled contingencies terminate, so does the behavior. Is this a real or pseudoproblem? How can the impact of this "side effect," if real, be dealt with?

Although much could be written about these questions and other questions could certainly be generated, they represent a selection of the loose ends in the field of behavior modification. Perhaps some of you will help to tie them up!

Appendix

	Contract Work Sheet	

Child _____

Teacher _____ Date _____

(X)	Tasks	Comments
( )	1. Establish and maintain rapport.	
( )	2. Explain the purpose of the meeting.	
( )	3. Explain a contract.	
( )	4. Give an example of a contract.	
( )	5. Ask the child to give an example of a contract; if there is no response, give another example.	
( )	6. Discuss possible tasks.	
( )	7. Child-suggested tasks: _____ _____ _____ _____	

Source: J. E. Walker and T. M. Shea. *Behavior Management: A Practical Approach for Educators* (3rd ed.) (Columbus, Ohio: Merrill, 1984). Copyright 1984 Merrill Publishing Company, Columbus, Ohio. Reprinted by permission of the publisher.

(X)	Tasks	Comments
( )	8. Teacher-suggested tasks: _____ _____ _____ _____	
( )	9. Agree on the task.	
( )	10. Ask the child what activities he or she enjoys and what items he or she wishes to possess.	
( )	11. Record child-suggested reinforcers.	
( )	12. Negotiate the ratio of the task to the reinforcer.	
( )	13. Identify the time allotted for the task.	
( )	14. Identify the criterion or achievement level.	
( )	15. Discuss methods of evaluation.	
( )	16. Agree on the method of evaluation.	
( )	17. Restate and clarify the method of evaluation.	
( )	18. Negotiate the delivery of the reinforcer.	
( )	19. Set the date for renegotiation.	
( )	20. Write two copies of the contract.	
( )	21. Read the contract to the child.	
( )	22. Elicit the child's verbal affirmation and give your own affirmation.	
( )	23. Sign the contract and have the child sign it.	
( )	24. Congratulate the child (and yourself).	

CONTRACT FORM*

Date _____

Contract

This is an agreement between _____
                                         Child's name

and _____ . The contract begins on
              Teacher's name

_____ and ends on _____ . It will be re-
          Date   Date

viewed on _____ .
                    Date

The terms of the agreement are:

Child will _____

_____

_____

_____

Teacher will _____

_____

_____

_____

   If the child fulfills his or her part of the contract, the child will receive the agreed-on reward from the teacher. However, if the child fails to fulfill his or her part of the contract, the rewards will be withheld.

Child's signature _____

Teacher's signature _____

*Source: J. E. Walker and T. M. Shea, *Behavior Management: A Practical Approach for Educators* (3rd ed.) (Columbus, Ohio: Merrill, 1984). Copyright 1984 Merrill Publishing Company, Columbus, Ohio. Reprinted by permission of the publisher.

ACTUAL CLIENT CONTRACTS

Jane R. is a 15-year-old girl. She has been arguing with her parents for several months about the excessive amount of time they say she spends on the telephone and the condition of her room. Before the development of the following nego-tiated contract, Jane noncontingently received approximately $10 a week from her parents.

Home Contract

Parties Involved: Jane R., Mr. and Mrs. R., and
                  Dr. William Sherman

1. Telephone:

    a. Jane will limit both her in-coming and out-going telephone calls to the hours of 9:00–10:30 P.M.
    b. Jane will return the telephone to her parents' room at 10:30 P.M.
    c. If these rules are adhered to for an entire week, Jane will earn the sum of $4. If, at any time, these rules are not adhered to, Jane will forfeit the $4.

2. Room:

    a. Jane will make her bed daily soon after she awakens in the morning.
    b. Jane will not leave any food, plates, cups, etc. in her room over-night.
    c. If these rules are adhered to for an entire week, Jane will earn the sum of $4. If, at any time, these rules are not adhered to, Jane will forfeit the $4.

3. For any week in which Jane earns the sum of $8, an additional $2 will be given as a bonus.

4. Jane will put her dirty laundry in the hamper in the bathroom; Mrs. R. will only wash clothes in the hamper.

5. The parties involved will mutually agree on the "first" and "last" days of a "week" and the time of day payment will be made.

6. Except for lunch money for school, Jane will generally not be given any money except what is earned on this contract.

7. Dr. Sherman will be contacted in the event of any questions or problems prior to the next appointment.

8. *Signed* and *dated:*

Tony B. is a 12-year-old, sixth-grade boy. His parents had been complaining about his "lack of responsibility" regarding his schoolwork. He frequently failed to write down his assignments, "forgot" to bring his books home, or simply didn't do his homework. This led to numerous arguments at home and also began to affect his grades adversely. The following negotiated contract involved the cooperation of Tony, his parents, and his classroom teacher.

Home/School Contract

Parties Involved: Tony B., Mr. & Mrs. B., classroom teacher, and
        Dr. William Sherman

1. Tony will show his homework to his teacher each morning shortly after he arrives at school. If it is complete (not necessarily correct), the teacher will award him a "point."

2. At the end of the school day, the teacher will check Tony's homework assignment pad. If it is complete and correct, the teacher will award him a point. If it is not complete or correct, Tony will have to redo it at that time but he will forfeit his point.

3. At the end of the school day, the teacher will see whether Tony has all the necessary books and/or papers out on his desk and ready to go home. If he does, the teacher will award him a point. If he does not, he will have to assemble the missing material at that time but he will forfeit his point.

4. Tony understands that under the terms of this contract, he could earn as many as 15 points per week. All points will be brought home at the end of each day and saved.

5. At home, over the weekend, Tony will "cash in" his accumulated points for that week. Reinforcers will be chosen from a "menu" he has made with the help of his parents and Dr. Sherman.

6. Dr. Sherman will be contacted in the event of any questions or problems before the next appointment.

7. *Signed* and *dated:*

References

Adubato, S. A., Adams, M. K., & Budd, K. S. (1981). Teaching a parent to train a spouse in child management techniques. *Journal of Applied Behavior Analysis, 14,* 193–205.

Agras, W. S., & Berkowitz, R. (1980). Clinical research in behavior therapy: Half-way there? *Behavior Therapy, 11,* 472–487.

Aiken, J. M., & Salzberg, C. L. (1984). The effects of a sensory extinction procedure on stereotypic sounds of two autistic children. *Journal of Autism and Developmental Disorders, 14,* 291–299.

American Psychiatric Association. (1979). *Diagnostic and statistical manual of mental disorders* (3rd ed.). Washington, D.C.

American Psychiatric Association. (1987). *Diagnostic and statistical manual of mental disorders* (3rd ed., revised). Washington, D.C.

Association for Advancement of Behavior Therapy. (1977). Ethical issues for human services. *Behavior Therapy, 8,* 763–764.

Axelrod, S. (1977). *Behavior modification for the classroom teacher.* New York: McGraw-Hill.

Ayllon, T., & Azrin, N. (1968). *The token economy: A motivational system for therapy and rehabilitation.* Englewood Cliffs, N.J.: Prentice-Hall.

Ayllon, T., Layman, D., & Kandel, H. J. (1975). A behavioral education alternative to drug control of hyperactive children. *Journal of Applied Behavior Analysis, 8,* 137–146.

Azrin, N. H., & Foxx, R. M. (1974). *Toilet training in less than a day.* New York: Simon & Schuster.

Azrin, N. H., & Holz, W. C. (1966). Punishment. In W. K. Honig (Ed.), *Operant behavior: Areas of research and application.* Englewood Cliffs, N.J.: Prentice-Hall.

Azrin, N. H., & Thienes, P. M. (1978). Rapid elimination of enuresis by intensive learning without a conditioning apparatus. *Behavior Therapy, 9,* 342–354.

Bacon-Prue, A., Blount, R., Hosey, C., & Drabman, R. S. (1980). The public posting of photographs as a reinforcer for bedmaking in an institutional setting. *Behavior Therapy, 11,* 417–420.

Baile, W. F., & Engel, B. T. (1978). A behavioral strategy for promoting treatment compliance following myocardial infarction. *Psychosomatic Medicine, 40,* 413–419.

Bandura, A. (1969). *Principles of behavior modification.* New York: Holt, Rinehart and Winston.

Barlow, D. H. (1980). Behavior therapy: The next decade. *Behavior Therapy, 11,* 315–328.

Barmann, B. C., Croyle-Barmann, C., & McLain, B. (1980). The use of contingent-interrupted music in the treatment of disruptive bus-riding behavior. *Journal of Applied Behavior Analysis, 13,* 693–698.

Barton, E. S., Guess, D., Garcia E., & Baer, D. M. (1970). Improvement of retar-dates' mealtime behaviors by time-out procedures using multiple base-line techniques. *Journal of Applied Behavior Analysis, 3,* 77–84.

Bates, P., & Wehman, P. (1977). Behavior management with the mentally retarded: An empirical analysis of the research. *Mental Retardation, 15,* 9–12.

Beck, A. & Emery, G. (1985). *Anxiety disorders and phobias: A cognitive perspective.* New York: Basic Books.

Begelman, D. A. (1976). Ethical and legal issues of behavior modification. In M. Hersen, R. M. Eisler, & P. H. Miller (Eds.), *Progressive behavior modification* (Vol. 1). New York: Academic Press.

Bellack, A. S., & Hersen, M. (1977). *Behavior modification: An introductory text-book.* New York: Oxford University Press.

Bennett, D. (1980). Elimination of habitual vomiting using DRO procedures. *The Behavior Therapist, 3,* 16–18.

Berni, R., & Fordyce, W. E. (1977). *Behavior modification and the nursing process* (2nd ed.). St. Louis: Mosby.

Bernstein, D. A., & Glasgow, R. E. (1979). Smoking. In O. F. Pomerleau & J. P. Brady (Eds.), *Behavioral medicine: Theory and practice.* Baltimore: Williams & Wilkins.

Bijou, S. W., & Baer, D. M. (1961). *Child development I: A systematic and empiri-cal theory.* Englewood Cliffs, N.J.: Prentice-Hall.

Black, A. H., Cott, A., & Pavloski, R. (1977). The operant learning theory approach to biofeedback training. In G. E. Schwartz & J. Beatty (Eds.), *Biofeedback: Theory and research.* New York: Academic Press.

Blanchard, E. B., McCoy, G. C., Musso, A., Gerardi, M. A., Pallmeyer, T. P., Gerardi, R. J., Cotch, P. A., Siracusa, K., & Andrasik, F. (1986). A controlled comparison of thermal biofeedback and relaxation training in the treatment of essential hypertension: I. Short-term and long-term outcome. *Behavior Therapy, 17,* 563–579.

Blount, R. L, Baer, R. A., & Collins, R. L., Jr. (1984). Improving visual acuity in a myopic child: Assessing compliance and effectiveness. *Behaviour Research and Therapy, 22,* 53–57.

Bornstein, P. H., & Rychtarik, R. G. (1983). Consumer satisfaction in adult behavior therapy: Procedures, problems and future perspectives. *Behavior Therapy, 14,* 191–208.

Bourdon, R. D. (1977). A token economy application to management performance improvement. *Journal of Organizational Behavior Management, 1,* 23–37.

Broskowski, A. (1981). The health-mental health connection: An introduction. In A. Broskowski, E. Marks, & S. H. Budman (Eds.), *Linking health and mental health services.* Beverly Hills, Calif.: Sage.

Brown, D. M., Fugua, J. W., & Otts, D. A. (1986). Helping reluctant readers "stick" to it. *Academic Therapy, 21,* 599–604.

Browning, R. M., & Stover, D. O. (1971). *Behavior modification in child treatment: An experimental and clinical approach.* Chicago: Aldine.

Burchard, J. D., & Barrera, F. (1972). An analysis of time-out and response cost in a programmed environment. *Journal of Applied Behavior Analysis, 5,* 271–282.

Burgio, L. D., Page, R. J., & Capriotti, R. M. (1985). Clinical behavioral pharmacology: Methods for evaluating medications and contingency management. *Journal of Applied Behavior Analysis, 18,* 45–59.

Burton, B. T., & Foster, W. R. (1985). Health implications of obesity: An NIH consensus development conference. *Journal of the American Dietetic Association, 85,* 1117–1121.

Calvert, S. C., & McMahon, R. J. (1987). The treatment acceptability of a behavioral parent training program and its components. *Behavior Therapy, 18,* 165–179.

Carden Smith, L. K., & Fowler, S. A. (1984). Positive peer pressure: The effects of peer monitoring on children's disruptive behavior. *Journal of Applied Behavior Analysis, 17,* 213–227.

Carney, R. M., Schechter, K., & Davis, T. (1983). Improving adherence to blood glucose testing in insulin-dependent diabetic children. *Behavior Therapy, 14,* 247–254.

Cautela, J. R. (1977). *Behavior analysis forms for clinical intervention* (Vol. 1). Champaign, Ill.: Research Press.

Cautela, J. R. (1981). *Behavior analysis forms for clinical intervention* (Vol. 2). Champaign, Ill.: Research Press.

Chaney, E. F., O'Leary, M. R., & Marlatt, G. A. (1978). Skill training with alcoholics. *Journal of Consulting and Clinical Psychology, 46,* 1092–1104.

Claerhout, S., & Lutzker, J. R. (1981). Increasing children's self-initiated compliance to dental regimens. *Behavior Therapy, 12,* 165–176.

Clark, H. B., Greene, B. F., Macrae, J. W., McNees, M. P., Davis, J. L., & Risley, T. R. (1977). A parent advice package for family shopping trips: Development and evaluation. *Journal of Applied Behavior Analysis, 10,* 605–624.

Clark, L. (1986). Time-out! Instruction by videotape. *The Behavior Therapist, 9,* 151.

Clark, R. N., Burgess, R. L., & Hendee, J. C. (1972). The development of antilitter behavior in a forest campground. *Journal of Applied Behavior Analysis, 5,* 1–5.

Craighead, W. E., Kazdin, A. E., & Mahoney, M. J. (1981). *Behavior modification: Principles, issues, and applications.* Boston: Houghton Mifflin.

Dachman, R. S., Halasz, M. M., & Bickett, A. D. (1984). The use of dot-to-dot posters and a grab-bag to reduce inappropriate child behavior. *The Behavior Therapist, 7,* 4.

Dapcich-Miura, E., & Hovell, M. F. (1979). Contingency management of adherence to a complex medical regimen in an elderly heart patient. *Behavior Therapy, 10,* 193–201.

Davis, J. R., Wallace, C. J., Liberman, R. P. & Finch, B. E. (1976). The use of brief isolation to suppress delusional and hallucinatory speech. *Journal of Behavior Therapy and Experimental Psychiatry, 7,* 269–276.

Deci, E. L. (1971). Effects of externally mediated rewards on intrinsic motivation. *Journal of Personality and Social Psychology, 18,* 105–115.

DeLuca, R. V., & Holborn, S. W. (1985). Effects of a fixed interval schedule of token reinforcement on exercise with obese and non-obese boys. *The Psychological Record, 35,* 525–533.

Dorsey, M. F., Iwata, B. A., Ong, P., & McSween, T. E. (1980). Treatment of self-injurious behavior using a water mist: Initial response suppression and generalization. *Journal of Applied Behavior Analysis, 13,* 343–353.

Edelson, S. M., Taubman, M. T., & Lovaas, O. I. (1983). Some social contexts of self-destructive behavior. *Journal of Abnormal Child Psychology, 11,* 299–312.

Edelstein, B. A., & Eisler, R. M. (1976). Effects of modeling and modeling with instructions and feedback on the behavioral components of social skills. *Behavior Therapy, 7,* 382–389.

Ellis, A. & Harper, R. A. (1975). *A new guide to rational living.* Englewood Cliffs, N.J.: Prentice-Hall.

Elwood, D. L. (1975). Automation methods. In F. H. Kanfer & A. P. Goldstein (Eds.), *Helping people change: A textbook of methods.* Elmsford, N.Y.: Pergamon Press.

Everett, P. B., Hayward, S. C., & Meyer, A. W. (1974). Effects of a token reinforcement procedure on bus ridership. *Journal of Applied Behavior Analysis, 7,* 1–9.

Fairchild, T. (1985). A home-school token economy plan. *Elementary School Guidance and Counseling, 20,* 141–146.

Fimian, M. J. (1980). A table-top duration/frequency recording device. *The Behavior Therapist, 3,* 22.

Fordyce, W. E., & Steger, J. C. (1979). Chronic pain. In O. F. Pomerleau & J. P. Brady (Eds.), *Behavioral medicine: Theory and practice.* Baltimore: Williams & Wilkins.

Forman, S. (1980). A comparison of cognitive training and response cost procedures in modifying aggressive behavior of elementary school children. *Behavior Therapy, 11,* 594–600.

Foxx, R. M., & Azrin, N. H. (1972). Restitution: A method of eliminating aggressive-disruptive behavior of mentally retarded and brain damaged patients. *Behaviour Research and Therapy, 10,* 15–27.

Foxx, R. M., McMorrow, M. J., Bittle, R. G., & Bechtel, D. R. (1986). The successful treatment of a dually-diagnosed deaf man's aggression with a program that included contingent electric shock. *Behavior Therapy, 17,* 170–186.

Fuller, P. R. (1949). Operant conditioning of a vegetative human organism. *American Journal of Psychology, 62,* 587–590.

Furman, W., Geller, M., Simon, S. J., & Kelly, J. A. (1979). The use of a behavior rehearsal procedure for teaching job-interviewing skills to psychiatric patients. *Behavior Therapy, 10,* 157–167.

Gambrill, E. D. (1977). *Behavior modification: Handbook of assessment, intervention, and evaluation.* San Francisco: Jossey-Bass.

Gardner, J. M. (1975). Training nonprofessionals in behavior modification. In T. Thompson & W. S. Dockens, III (Eds.), *Applications of behavior modification.* New York: Academic Press.

Greene, B. F., Bailey, J. S., & Barber, F. (1981). An analysis and reduction of disruptive behavior on school buses. *Journal of Applied Behavior Analysis, 14,* 177–192.

Griffiths, R. R., Bigelow, G., & Liebson, I. (1977). Comparison of social time-out and activity time-out procedures in suppressing ethanol self-administration in alcoholics. *Behaviour Research and Therapy, 15,* 329–336.

Hall, J. N., Baker, R. D., & Hutchinson, K. (1977). A controlled evaluation of token economy procedures with chronic schizophrenic patients. *Behaviour Research and Therapy, 15,* 261–283.

Halmi, K. A., Powers, P., & Cunningham, S. (1975). Treatment of anorexia nervosa with behavior modification. *Archives of General Psychiatry, 32,* 93–97.

Harlow, H. F. (1958). The nature of love. *American Psychologist, 13,* 673–685.

Hart, B., Reynolds, N., Baer, D., Brawley, E., & Harris, F. (1968). Effect of contingent and noncontingent social reinforcement on the cooperative play of a preschool child. *Journal of Applied Behavior Analysis, 1,* 73–76.

Hartwell, S. L., Kaplan, R. M., & Wallace, J. P. (1986). Comparison of behavioral interventions for control of Type II diabetes mellitus. *Behavior Therapy, 17,* 447–461.

Haynes, S. N. (1978). *Principles of behavioral assessment.* New York: Gardner Press.

Heller, R. F., & Strang, H. R. (1973). Controlling bruxism through automated aversive conditioning. *Behaviour Research and Therapy, 11,* 327–329.

Hermann, J. A., deMontes, A. I., Dominguez, B., Montes, F., & Hopkins, B. L. (1973). Effects of bonuses for punctuality on the tardiness of industrial workers. *Journal of Applied Behavior Analysis, 6,* 563–572.

Hobbs, S. A., Walle, D. L., & Caldwell, H. S. (1984). Maternal evaluation of social reinforcement on time-out: Effects of brief parent training. *Journal of Consulting and Clinical Psychology, 52,* 135–136.

Hogan, W. A., & Johnson, D. P. (1985). Elimination of response cost in a token economy program and improvement in behavior of emotionally disturbed youth. *Behavior Therapy, 16,* 87–98.

Hollander, M., & Plutchik, R. (1972). A reinforcement program for psychiatric attendants. *Journal of Behavior Therapy and Experimental Psychiatry, 3,* 297–300.

Hollon, S. D., & Beck, A. T. (1979). Cognitive therapy of depression. In P. C. Kendall & S. D. Hollon (Eds.), *Cognitive-behavioral interventions: Theory, research, and procedures.* New York: Academic Press.

Holt, M. M., & Hobbs, T. R. (1979). The effects of token reinforcement, feedback and response cost on standardized test performance. *Behaviour Research and Therapy, 17,* 81–83.

Homer, A. L., & Peterson, L. (1980). Differential reinforcement of other behavior: A preferred response elimination procedure. *Behavior Therapy, 11,* 449–471.

Homme, L. E., deBaca, P. C., Devine, J. V., Steinhorst, R., & Rickert, E. J. (1963). Use of the Premack principle in controlling the behavior of nursery school children. *Journal of the Experimental Analysis of Behavior, 6,* 544.

Hull, C. L. (1943). *Principles of behavior.* Englewood Cliffs, N.J.: Prentice-Hall.

Isaacs, W., Thomas, J., & Goldiamond, I. (1960). Application of operant conditioning to reinstate verbal behavior in psychotics. *Journal of Speech and Hearing Disorders, 25,* 8–12.

Iwata, B. A., & Becksfort, C. M. (1981). Behavioral research in preventive dentistry: Education and contingency management approaches to the problem of patient compliance. *Journal of Applied Behavior Analysis, 14,* 111–120.

Jackson, J., Carlson, C. L., & Treiber, F. A. (1987). Outpatient behavioral treatment of obesity in a child with Prader-Willi syndrome. *Journal of Child and Adolescent Psychotherapy, 4,* 116–120.

Jacobson, N. S., & Anderson, E. A. (1980). The effects of behavior rehearsal and feedback on the acquisition of problem-solving skills in distressed and nondistressed couples. *Behaviour Research and Therapy, 18,* 25–36.

James, J. E. (1981). Behavioral self-control of stuttering using time-out from speaking. *Journal of Applied Behavior Analysis, 14,* 25–37.

Jason, L. A. (1984). Reducing excessive television viewing among seven children in one family. *The Behavior Therapist, 7,* 3–4.

Jayaratne, S. (1978). A study of clinical eclecticism. *Social Service Review, 52,* 621–631.

Johnson, W. G., & Corrigan, S. A. (1987). The behavioral treatment of child and adolescent obesity. *Journal of Child and Adolescent Psychotherapy, 4,* 91–100.

The Joint National Committee on Detection, Evaluation, and Treatment of High Blood Pressure. (1984). The 1984 report. *Archives of Internal Medicine, 144,* 1045–1057.

Kagel, J. H., & Winkler, R. C. (1972). Behavioral economics: Areas of cooperative research between economics and applied behavioral analysis. *Journal of Applied Behavior Analysis, 5,* 335–342.

Kanfer, F. H., & Phillips, J. S. (1970). *Learning foundations of behavior therapy.* New York: Wiley.

Katz, R. C., & Vinciguerra, P. (1982). On the neglected art of "thinning" reinforcers. *The Behavior Therapist, 5,* 21–22.

Kazdin, A. E. (1977). *The token economy: A review and evaluation.* New York: Plenum.

Kazdin, A. E. (1978). *History of behavior modification: Experimental foundations of contemporary research.* Baltimore: University Park Press.

Kazdin, A. E. (1980). Acceptability of time out from reinforcement procedures for disruptive child behavior. *Behavior Therapy, 11,* 329–344.

Kazdin, A. E., & Mascitelli, S. (1980). The opportunity to earn oneself off a token system as a reinforcer for attentive behavior. *Behavior Therapy, 11,* 68–78.

Kendall, P. C., & Hollon, S. D. (1979). Cognitive-behavioral interventions: Overview and current status. In P. C. Kendall & S. D. Hollon (Eds.), *Cognitive-behavioral interventions: Theory, research, and procedures.* New York: Academic Press.

Kish, G. B. (1966). Studies of sensory reinforcement. In W. K. Honig (Ed.), *Operant behavior: Areas of research and application.* Englewood Cliffs, N.J.: Prentice-Hall.

Krueger, J. R. (1961). An early instance of conditioning from the Chinese dynastic histories. *Psychological Reports, 9,* 117.

LaDouceur, R., & Auger, J. (1980). Where have all the follow-ups gone? *The Behavior Therapist, 3,* 10–11.

Levine, F. M., & Fasnacht, G. (1974). Token rewards may lead to token learning. *American Psychologist, 29,* 816–820.

Levy, R. L. (1987). Compliance and clinical practice. In J. A. Blumenthal & D. C. McKee (Eds.), *Applications in behavioral medicine and health psychology: A clinician's source book.* Sarasota, Fla.: Professional Resource Exchange.

Lovitt, T. C., & Hansen, C. L. (1976). The use of contingent skipping and drilling to improve oral reading and comprehension. *Journal of Learning Disabilities, 9,* 481–487.

Lubar, J. F., & Shouse, M. N. (1977). Use of biofeedback in the treatment of hyperactivity. In B. B. Lahey & A. E. Kazdin (Eds.), *Advances in clinical child psychology* (Vol. 1). New York: Plenum.

Luce, S. C., Delquadri, J., & Hall, R. V. (1980). Contingent exercise: A mild but powerful procedure for suppressing inappropriate verbal and aggressive behavior. *Journal of Applied Behavior Analysis, 13,* 583–594.

Lutzker, J. R., & Martin, J. A. (1981). *Behavior change.* Monterey, Calif.: Brooks/Cole.

McAllister, L. W., Stachowiak, J. G., Baer, D. M., & Conderman, L. (1969). The application of operant conditioning techniques in a secondary school classroom. *Journal of Applied Behavior Analysis, 2,* 277–285.

McCaul, M. E., Stitzer, M. L., Bigelow, G. E., & Liebson, I. A. (1984). Contingency management interventions: Effects on treatment outcome during methadone detoxification. *Journal of Applied Behavior Analysis, 17,* 35–43.

Mace, F. C., Page, T. J., Ivancic, M. T., & O'Brien, S. (1986). Effectiveness of brief time-out with and without contingent delay: A comparative analysis. *Journal of Applied Behavior Analysis, 19,* 79–86.

McReynolds, W. T. (1979). DSM–III and the future of applied social science. *Professional Psychology, 10,* 123–132.

Madsen, C. H., Becker, W. C., Thomas, D. R., Koser, L., & Plager, E. (1970). An analysis of the reinforcing function of "sit down" commands. In R. K. Parker (Ed.), *Readings in educational psychology.* Boston: Allyn & Bacon.

Mahoney, M. J. (1977). Reflections on the cognitive-learning trend in psychotherapy. *American Psychologist, 32,* 5–13.

Marlatt, G. A., & George, W. H. (1984). Relapse prevention: Introduction and overview of the model. *British Journal of Addiction, 79,* 261–273.

Martin, G. L., Kehoe, B., Bird, E., Jensen, V., & Darbyshire, M. (1971). Operant conditioning in dressing behavior of severely retarded girls. *Mental Retardation, 9,* 27–31.

Martin, G., & Pear, J. (1978). *Behavior modification: What it is and how to do it.* Englewood Cliffs, N.J.: Prentice-Hall.

Martin, G., & Pear, J. (1983). *Behavior modification: What it is and how to do it* (2nd ed.). Englewood Cliffs, N.J.: Prentice-Hall.

Martin, M., Burkholder, R., Rosenthal, T., Tharp, R., & Thorne, G. (1968). Programming behavior change and reintegration into school milieux of extreme adolescent deviates. *Behaviour Research and Therapy, 6,* 371–383.

Martin, R. (1975). *Legal challenges to behavior modification: Trends in schools, corrections, and mental health.* Champaign, Ill.: Research Press.

Mash, E. J., Hamerlynck, L. A., & Handy, L. C. (Eds.). (1976). *Behavior modification and families.* New York: Brunner/Mazel.

Mash, E. J., Handy, L. C., & Hamerlynck, L. A. (Eds.). (1976). *Behavior modification approaches to parenting.* New York: Brunner/Mazel.

Matesanz, A. (1982). Auditory stimuli in aversion therapy: A new technique. *The Behavior Therapist, 5,* 25–26.

Matson, J. L. (1980). Behavior modification procedures for training chronically institutionalized schizophrenics. In M. Hersen, R. M. Eisler, & P. M. Miller (Eds.), *Progress in behavior modification* (Vol. 9). New York: Academic Press.

Mayer, J. A., Dubbert, P. M., Scott, R. R., Dawson, B. L., Ekstrand, M. L., & Fondren, T. G. (1987). Breast self-examination: The effects of personalized prompts on practice frequency. *Behavior Therapy, 18,* 135–146.

Meredith, R. L., & Milby, J. B. (1980). Obsessive-compulsive disorders. In R. J. Daitzman (Ed.), *Clinical behavior therapy and behavior modification* (Vol. 1). New York: Garland STPM Press.

Meyers, H., Nathan, P. E., & Kopel, S. (1977). Effects of a token reinforcement system on journal reshelving. *Journal of Applied Behavior Analysis, 10,* 213–218.

Milberg, W. P., & Hebben, N. A. (1979). Termination of self-monitoring as a negative reinforcer to increase weight gain in a 77-year-old anorexic male. *The Behavior Therapist, 2,* 21–22.

Miller, A. J., & Kratochwill, T. R. (1979). Reduction of frequent stomachache complaints by time out. *Behavior Therapy, 10,* 211–218.

Miller, N. E. (1969). Learning of visceral and glandular responses. *Science, 163,* 434–445.

Miller, N. E. (1985). Some professional and scientific problems and opportunities for biofeedback. *Biofeedback and Self-Regulation, 10,* 3–24.

Morris, R. J., & Kratochwill, T. R. (1983). *Treating children's fears and phobias.* Elmsford, N.Y.: Pergamon Press.

Moss, G. R., & Rick, G. R. (1981a). Application of a token economy for adolescents in a private psychiatric hospital. *Behavior Therapy, 12,* 585–590.

Moss, G. R., & Rick, G. R. (1981b). Overview: Applications of operant technology to behavioral disorders of adolescents. *American Journal of Psychiatry, 138,* 1161–1169.

Murphy, G., & Goddall, E. (1980). Measurement error in direct observations: A comparison of common recording methods. *Behaviour Research and Therapy, 18,* 147–150.

Neuringer, A. J. (1969). Animals respond for food in the presence of free food. *Science, 166,* 399–401.

Noonberg, A. R. (1985). Biofeedback training: Offerings, plans, and some attitudes in graduate schools and internships. *Biofeedback and Self-Regulation, 10,* 25–32.

O'Leary, K. D. (1984). The image of behavior therapy: It is time to take a stand. *Behavior Therapy, 15,* 219–233.

O'Leary, K. D., Becker, W. C., Evans, M. B., & Saudargas, R. A. (1969). A token reinforcement program in a public school: A replication and systematic analysis. *Journal of Applied Behavior Analysis, 2,* 3–13.

O'Leary, K. D., Pelham, W. E., Rosenbaum, A., & Price, G. H. (1976). Behavioral treatment of hyperkinetic children: An experimental evaluation of its usefulness. *Clinical Pediatrics, 15,* 510–515.

Olton, D. S., & Noonberg, A. R. (1980). *Biofeedback: Clinical applications in behavioral medicine.* Englewood Cliffs, N.J.: Prentice-Hall.

Patterson, R. L., & Jackson, G. M. (1980). Behavior modification with the elderly. In M. Hersen, R. M. Eisler, & P. M. Miller (Eds.), *Progress in behavior modification* (Vol. 9). New York: Academic Press.

Perri, M. G., McAdoo, W. G., McAllister, D. A., Lauer, J. B., & Yancey, D. Z. (1986). Enhancing the efficacy of behavior therapy for obesity: Effects of aerobic exercise and a multicomponent maintenance program. *Journal of Consulting and Clinical Psychology, 54,* 670–675.

Peters, H. N. (1952). An experimental evaluation of learning as therapy in schizophrenia. *American Psychologist, 7,* 354.

Peters, H. N. (1955). Learning as a treatment method in chronic schizophrenia. *The American Journal of Occupational Therapy, 9,* 185–189.

Pitts, C. E. (1976). Behavior modification—1787. *Journal of Applied Behavior Analysis, 9,* 146.

Pollock, D. D., & Liberman, R. P. (1974). Behavior therapy of incontinence in demented inpatients. *The Gerontologist, 14,* 488–491.

Pomerleau, O. F., & Brady, J. P. (1979). Introduction: The scope and promise of behavioral medicine. In O. F. Pomerleau & J. P. Brady (Eds.), *Behavioral medicine: Theory and practice.* Baltimore: Williams & Wilkins.

Premack, D. (1962). Reversibility of the reinforcement relation. *Science, 136,* 255–257.

Quay, H. C., Routh, D. K., & Shapiro, S. K. (1987). Psychopathology of childhood: From description to validation. In M. R. Rosenzweig & L. W. Porter (Eds.), *Annual Review of Psychology.* Palo Alto, Calif.: Annual Reviews.

Quilitch, H. R. (1978). Using a simple feedback procedure to reinforce the submission of written suggestions by mental health employees. *Journal of Organizational Behavior Management, 1,* 155–163.

Redd, W. & Sleator, W. (1976). *Take charge: A comprehensive analysis of behavior modification.* New York: Vintage Books.

Redmon, W. K. (1987). Reduction of physical attacks through differential reinforcement of other behavior. *Journal of Child and Adolescent Psychotherapy, 4,* 107–111.

Reynolds, G. S. (1968). *A primer of operant conditioning.* Glenview, Ill.: Scott, Foresman.

Reynolds, W. M., & Coats, K. I. (1986). A comparison of cognitive-behavioral therapy and relaxation training for the treatment of depression in adolescents. *Journal of Consulting and Clinical Psychology, 54,* 653–660.

Rimm, D. C., & Masters, J. C. (1979). *Behavior therapy: Techniques and empirical findings* (2nd ed.). New York: Academic Press.

Rincover, A., & Newsom, C. D. (1985). The relative motivational properties of sensory and edible reinforcers in teaching autistic children. *Journal of Applied Behavior Analysis, 18,* 237–248.

Risley, T. R., & Sheldon-Wildgen, J. (1980). Suggested procedures for human rights committees of potentially controversial treatment programs. *The Behavior Therapist, 3,* 9–10.

Roberts, A. H. (1985). Biofeedback: Research, training, and clinical roles. *American Psychologist, 40,* 938–941.

Roberts, M. C., & Fanurik, D. (1986). Rewarding elementary school children for their use of safety belts. *Health Psychology, 5,* 185–196.

Roberts, M. W., Hatzenbuehler, L. C., & Bean, A. W. (1981). The effects of differential attention and time out on child noncompliance. *Behavior Therapy, 12,* 93–99.

Rolider, A., & VanHouten, R. (1985). Movement suppression time-out for undesirable behavior in psychotic and severely developmentally delayed children. *Journal of Applied Behavior Analysis, 18,* 275–288.

Rose, S. D. (1977). *Group therapy: A behavioral approach.* Englewood Cliffs, N.J.: Prentice-Hall.

Rose, S. D. (1980). *A casebook in group therapy: A behavioral-cognitive approach.* Englewood Cliffs, N.J.: Prentice-Hall.

Rosenhan, D. L. (1973). On being sane in insane places. *Science. 179,* 250–258.

Ross, A. O. (1981). *Child behavior therapy: Principles, procedures, and empirical basis.* New York: Wiley.

Ruprecht, M. J., Hanson, R. H., Pocrnich, M. A., & Murphy, R. J. (1980). Some suggested precautions when using lemon juice (citric acid) in behavior modification programs. *The Behavior Therapist, 3,* 12.

Sachs, D. A. (1973). The efficacy of time-out procedures in a variety of behavior problems. *Journal of Behavior Therapy and Experimental Psychiatry, 4,* 237–242.

Sarason, I. G., Glaser, E. M., & Fargo, G. A. (1972). *Reinforcing productive classroom behavior.* New York: Behavioral Publications.

Schaefer, C. E., & Millman, H. L. (1981). *How to help children with common problems.* New York: Van Nostrand Reinhold.

Schmidt, G. W., & Ulrich, R. E. (1969). Effects of group contingent events upon classroom noise. *Journal of Applied Behavior Analysis, 2,* 171–180.

Schwartz, G., & Beatty, J. (Eds.). (1977). *Biofeedback: Theory and research.* New York: Academic Press.

Schwartz, G., & Weiss, S. (1977). What is behavioral medicine? *Psychosomatic Medicine, 39,* 377–381.

Seidner, M. L., & Kirschenbaum, D. S. (1980). Behavioral contracts: Effects of pretreatment information and intention statements. *Behavior Therapy, 11,* 689–698.

Shapiro, D., & Surwit, R. S. (1979). Biofeedback. In O. F. Pomerleau & J. P. Brady (Eds.), *Behavioral medicine: Theory and practice.* Baltimore: Williams & Wilkins.

Shelton, J. L., & Levy, R. L. (1981). A survey of the reported use of assigned homework activities in contemporary behavior therapy literature. *The Behavior Therapist, 4,* 13–14.

Shumaker, S. A., & Grunberg, N. E. (Eds.). (1986). Proceedings of the National Working Conference on Smoking Relapse. *Health Psychology, 5,* (Suppl.), whole issue.

Singh, D. (1970). Preference for bar pressing to obtain reward over freeloading in rats and children. *Journal of Comparative and Physiological Psychology, 73,* 320–327.

Singh, N. N., Dawson, M. J., & Gregory, P. R. (1980). Suppression of chronic hyperventilation using response-contingent aromatic ammonia. *Behavior Therapy, 11,* 561–566.

Skinner, B. F. (1938). *The behavior of organisms: An experimental analysis.* Englewood Cliffs, N.J.: Prentice-Hall.

Skinner, B. F. (1953). *Science and human behavior.* New York: Macmillan.

Sloane, R. B., Staples, F. R., Cristol, A. H., Yorkston, J. J., & Whipple, K. (1975). *Psychotherapy versus behavior therapy.* Cambridge, Mass.: Harvard University Press.

Smith, J. B., Madsen, C. H., & Cipani, E. C. (1981). The effects of observational session length, method of recording, and frequency of teacher behavior on reliability and accuracy of observational data. *Behavior Therapy, 12,* 565–569.

Snortum, J. R. (1976). Self-modification: Ben Franklin's pursuit of perfection. *Psychology Today, 9,* 80–83.

Speltz, M. L., Moore, J. E., & McReynolds, W. T. (1979). A comparison of standardized and group contingencies in a classroom setting. *Behavior Therapy, 10,* 219–226.

Stokes, T. F., & Kennedy, S. H. (1980). Reducing child uncooperative behavior during dental treatment through modeling and reinforcement. *Journal of Applied Behavior Analysis, 13,* 41–49.

Stunkard, A. J. & Berthold, H. C. (1985). What is behavior therapy? A very short description of behavioral weight control. *The American Journal of Clinical Nutrition, 41,* 821–823.

Tate, B. G., & Baroff, G. S. (1966). Aversive control of self-injurious behavior in a psychotic boy. *Behaviour Research and Therapy, 4,* 281–287.

Tennov, D. (1975). *Psychotherapy: The hazardous cure.* New York: Abelard-Schuman.

Tharp, R. G., & Wetzel, R. J. (1969). *Behavior modification in the natural environment.* New York: Academic Press.

Thorndike, E. L. (1911). *Animal intelligence.* New York: Macmillan.

Thyer, B. A. (1987a). Behavioral social work: An overview. *The Behavior Therapist, 10,* 131–134.

Thyer, B. A. (1987b). Contingency contracting to promote automobile safety belt use by students. *The Behavior Therapist, 10,* 150, 166.

Tryon, W. W. (1976). Models of behavior disorder: A formal analysis based on Wood's taxonomy of instrumental conditioning. *American Psychologist, 31,* 509–518.

Tulkin, S., & Frank, G. (1985). The changing role of psychologists in health maintenance organizations. *American Psychologist, 40,* 1125–1130.

Turkat, I. D., & Brantley, P. J. (1981). On the therapeutic relationship in behavior therapy. *The Behavior Therapist, 4,* 16–17.

Turkat, I. D., & Feuerstein, M. (1978). Behavior modification and the public misconception. *American Psychologist, 33,* 194.

Ullman, L. P., & Krasner, L. (Eds.). (1965). *Case studies in behavior modification.* New York: Holt, Rinehart & Winston.

Vingoe, F. J. (1980). The treatment of a chronic obsessive condition via reinforcement contingent upon success in response prevention. *Behaviour Research and Therapy, 18,* 212–217.

Wacker, D. P., Berg, W. K., Wiggins, B., Muldoon, M., & Cavanaugh, J. (1985). Evaluation of reinforcer preferences for profoundly handicapped students. *Journal of Applied Behavior Analysis, 18,* 173–178.

Wade, T. C., Baker, T. B., & Hartmann, D. P. (1979). Behavior therapists' self-reported views and practices. *The Behavior Therapist, 2,* 3–6.

Walen, S. R., Hauserman, N. M., & Lavin, P. J. (1977). *Clinical guide to behavior therapy.* Baltimore: Williams & Wilkins.

Walker, J. E., & Shea, T. M. (1980). *Behavior modification: A practical approach for educators.* St. Louis: Mosby.

Walker, J. E. & Shea, T. M. (1984). *Behavior management: A practical approach for educators* (3rd ed.). Columbus, Ohio: Merrill.

Watson, D. L., & Tharp, R. G. (1977). *Self-directed behavior: Self-modification for personal adjustment* (2nd ed.). Monterey, Calif.: Brooks/Cole.

Watson, J. B. (1913). Psychology as the behaviorist views it. *Psychological Review, 20,* 158–177.

Watson, J. B. (1924). *Behaviorism.* Chicago: University of Chicago Press.

Weisenberg, M. (1983). Pain and pain control. In R. J. Daitzman (Ed.), *Diagnosis and intervention in behavior therapy and behavioral medicine* (Vol. 1). New York: Springer-Verlag.

White, G. D., Nielsen, G., & Johnson, S. M. (1972). Timeout duration and suppression of deviant behavior in children. *Journal of Applied Behavior Analysis, 5,* 111–120.

White, M. D., & White, C. A. (1981). Involuntarily committed patients' constitutional right to refuse treatment: A challenge to psychology. *American Psychologist, 36,* 953–962.

Williams, C. (1959). The elimination of tantrum behavior by extinction procedures. *Journal of Abnormal and Social Psychology, 59,* 269.

Winkler, R. C. (1973). An experimental analysis of economic balance, savings and wages in a token economy. *Behavior Therapy, 4,* 22–40.

Witt, J. C., & Robbins, J. R. (1985). Acceptability of reductive interventions for the control of inappropriate child behavior. *Journal of Abnormal Child Psychology, 13,* 59–67.

Wolf, M., Birnbrauer, J., Lawler, J., & Williams, T. (1970). The operant extinction, reinstatement, and re-extinction of vomiting behavior in a retarded child. In R. Ulrich, T. Stachnik, & J. Mabry (Eds.), *Control of human behavior: From cure to prevention* (Vol. 2). Glenview, Ill.: Scott, Foresman.

Woods, P. J. (1974). A taxonomy of instrumental conditioning. *American Psychologist, 29,* 584–597.

Wright, D. F., Brown, R. A., & Andrews, M. E. (1978). Remission of chronic ruminative vomiting through a reversal of social contingencies. *Behaviour Research and Therapy, 16,* 134–136.

Wright, D. F., Slucki, H., & Benetti, B. (1983). Elimination of pain behavior in a burned child through a reversal of social contingencies. *Journal of the American Academy of Behavioral Medicine, 1,* 31–44.

Wulbert, M., & Dries, R. (1977). The relative efficacy of methylphenidate (ritalin) and behavior-modification techniques in the treatment of a hyperactive child. *Journal of Applied Behavior Analysis, 10,* 21–31.

Zubin, J. (1967). The classification of behavior disorders. *Annual Review of Psychology, 18,* 373–401.

Index